A Practical Guide to Mental Health Counseling

Cynthia J. Osborn
Kent State University

CENGAGE Learning

Australia • Brazil • Mexico • Singapore • United Kingdom • United States

CENGAGE
Learning

WCN: 01-100-101

ISBN: 978-1-305-40103-7

Cengage Learning
20 Channel Center Street
Boston, MA 02210
USA

Cengage Learning is a leading provider of customized learning solutions with office locations around the globe, including Singapore, the United Kingdom, Australia, Mexico, Brazil, and Japan. Locate your local office at: **www.cengage.com/global**.

Cengage Learning products are represented in Canada by Nelson Education, Ltd.

To learn more about Cengage Learning Solutions, visit **www.cengage.com**.

Purchase any of our products at your local college store or at our preferred online store **www.cengagebrain.com**.

Printed in the United States of America
Print Number: 01 Print Year: 2014

Contents

A PRACTICAL GUIDE TO MENTAL HEALTH COUNSELING

Cynthia J. Osborn
Kent State University

Mental health counseling (MHC) encompasses a wide range of services provided by a diverse group of professionals to an ever increasing consumer population in the United States today. The two fundamental and simultaneous purposes of MHC are to promote mental health and to prevent the worsening of symptoms associated with mental illness. This chapter is intended to provide an overview of MHC practices, providers, and service recipients (i.e., consumers, clients, or patients) as well as trends and current priorities in MHC. A brief history of MHC is provided and ethical and legal considerations are reviewed. Implications for the future of MHC are also considered, including preparation of MHC providers.

Clarification about terminology is necessary at the start of this chapter. Research on MHC does not always distinguish among services or providers. For example, Yu, Adams, Burns, Brindis, and Irwin (2008) studied the use of MHC among adolescents and young adults (using data from the National Longitudinal Study of Adolescent Health, sponsored by the National Institute of Child Health and Human Development, an agency of the National Institutes of Health). In this study, "mental health counseling" was defined as "psychological or emotional counseling" (p. 270) without reference to specific interventions or providers. Because MHC spans many different types of services (including psychopharmacological interventions), settings (e.g., schools, pharmacy walk-in clinics), and providers (including medical doctors, such as psychiatrists), this chapter takes a broad approach to MHC, not aligning it with any discipline or professional association (e.g., the American Counseling Association, ACA), nor confining MHC to one specific type of intervention (e.g., "talk therapy"). Such an approach is consistent with the trend in (indeed, the mandate of) collaborative and interdisciplinary mental health care (see Yeager, Cutler, Svendsen, & Sills, 2013).

What is Mental Health Counseling?

To understand the practice that is mental health counseling (MHC), it is important first to discuss *mental health*. If MHC is the promotion of mental health, what exactly is being promoted?

Mental Health

The first U.S. Surgeon General to issue a report on mental health was Dr. David Satcher. In his *Mental Health: A Report of the Surgeon General* (U.S. Department of Health and Human Services, U.S. DHHS,1999), mental health is defined as "a state of successful performance of mental function, resulting in productive activities, fulfilling relationships with other people, and the ability to adapt to change and to cope with adversity" (p. 4). Mental health is further characterized as "indispensable to personal well-being, family and interpersonal relationships, and contribution to community and society... [because it] is the springboard of thinking and communication skills, learning, emotional growth, resilience, and self-esteem" (p. 4). Although certainly not the first definition of mental health, this nontechnical definition is rather comprehensive and comprehensible. It suggests that mental health is synonymous with personal well-being expressed in family, community, and societal interactions, and is demonstrated in coping, adaptive, and resilient behavior.

This same report differentiates mental health from mental illness. The latter is defined as the collection of all diagnosable mental disorders, which are health conditions characterized by alterations in thinking, mood, or behavior associated with some distress and/or impaired functioning (U.S. DHHS, 1999). MHC therefore is intended to promote personal well-being or resilience *as well as* to arrest ongoing distress and to prevent further impairment. In this way MHC is salutary (or health-promoting) *and* remedial (or corrective). It is also appropriate for persons who do not have a mental illness: persons who are struggling in one or more areas of their life (e.g., dissatisfied with a current intimate relationship, ambivalent about career choice) whose own attempts at self-care have not been beneficial and whose struggles do not match or qualify as a mental disorder. Said in another way, MHC is not reserved only for persons with mental illness. It is used predominantly, however, for persons who do have diagnosable mental disorders. For example, in one study (Burns et al., 1995) of 1,015 children and adolescents (9-, 11-, and 13-year olds), only 1.6% without a diagnosis of a mental health condition used mental health services in the previous 3 months, compared to 21.6% with a diagnosis who used such services. Children and adolescents who participated in any type of mental health service were seen primarily (70-80%) by providers in the school setting, including guidance counselors and school psychologists.

Mental Health Counseling

The *practice* of mental health counseling (MHC) spans disciplines and professions. Just as the recipients or consumers of MHC are not exclusively persons with mental illness (although they are predominantly), the providers of MHC are not one group of professionals. Those trained in psychiatry, social work, psychology, nursing, and counseling—to name just a few—all provide MHC and their practice reflects the values, philosophy, and principles of their respective discipline. For example, psychiatry is one form of medicine and therefore medical intervention (e.g., medication) is a primary practice. Nursing is closely related to medicine with its focus of care primarily on physical health. One of the newest health care professions is counseling, which got its start in vocational guidance and thus has emphasized a range of methods (e.g., psychoeducation) to promote general health development across the lifespan. Distinctions among these professions are not always clear and some studies do not distinguish MHC from medical care (e.g., National Longitudinal Study of Adolescent Health data used by Yu et al., 2008).

Although MHC is not the practice of only one profession, it is viewed by many as a distinct profession linked to a professional association: the American Mental Health Counselors Association (AMHCA), a division of the ACA. One early definition of MHC assumes this link:

> Mental health counseling, a core mental health care profession, is the aggregate of the specific educational, scientific, and professional contributions of the disciplines of education, psychology, and counseling focused on promotion and maintenance of mental health, the prevention and treatment of mental illness, the identification and

> modification of etiologic, diagnostic, and systems correlates of mental health, mental illness, and related dysfunction, and the improvement of the mental health service delivery system. (Spruill & Fong, 1990, pp. 20-21)

This definition highlights the interdisciplinary history of MHC. It also reflects the dramatic shifts in the views and practice of MHC over the years. Historically, MHC referred to non-school counseling (i.e., counseling that was not "guidance counseling") that used non-medical approaches to psychotherapy provided in the community (Fong, 1990; Weikel & Palmo, 1989). This view has since changed as many community-based MHC facilities now contract with K-12 schools to supply mental health care providers to work with students and families in the school setting. But MHC should not be defined strictly according to setting of practice. Again, MHC spans settings, disciplines, and professions, thereby making its depiction as a "kaleidoscope" particularly apt (Glosoff & Schwarz-Whittaker, 2013, p. 31).

To add further "color" or complexity to this "kaleidoscope" that is MHC is the use of the term psychotherapy. Nystul (2011) differentiates counseling from psychotherapy, with the former on one end of a continuum of mental health care and psychotherapy on the other end. He describes counseling as serving a "growth facilitative" role (p. 7) that is preventive and developmental in nature and addresses immediate conscious processes. He states that counseling approaches are usually short-term and are "more appropriate for clients who have 'problems of living,' such as parent-child conflicts or marital difficulties" (p. 7). This seems consistent with the "'counseling' style" described by Davis and Biltz (1998, p. 239): it is care that "is highly individualized and is designed to facilitate problem solving and/or to enhance the patient and family coping resources so that relevant information, feedback, and support is effective."

Compared to counseling, Nystul (2011) states that psychotherapy addresses unconscious processes, is usually long-term, and has a remedial emphasis in that it helps clients "overcome the pain and suffering associated with existing problems, such as anxiety and depression" (p. 7). It seems, however, that there has been a lack of an agreed-upon definition of psychotherapy for quite some time (see Vessey & Howard, 1990) and Nystul acknowledges that counseling and psychotherapy are really more similar than different. Indeed, these practices often are equated in research (e.g., Olfson & Marcus, 2010) without clarifying the types of services provided in one or the other (e.g., Rosen et al., 2011).

In the Medical Expenditure Panel Survey (MEPS), MHC and psychotherapy are used interchangeably. The MEPS is a set of large-scale national surveys launched in 1996, sponsored by the Agency for Healthcare Research and Quality (a part of the U.S. DHHS), that periodically collects data on specific health services Americans use, including how frequently they use them and the cost of these services (see http://meps.ahrq.gov). Questionnaires used in MEPS define MHC (also referred to as psychotherapy) as:

> A treatment technique for certain forms of mental disorders relying principally on verbal communications between the mental health professional and the patient. [MHC] [c]an be individual, family, and/or group therapies… [and includes] care provided by any type of health professional so long as treatment is for **mental**

> health. [It] [d]oes **not** include visits with clergy to discuss personal problems. Any other professional mental health therapist such as a psychiatrist, psychologist, counselor, social worker, etc. would be included. (bold type in the original; see Glossary at http://meps.ahrq.gov)

This definition reinforces the longstanding interdisciplinary nature of MHC and regards counseling and psychotherapy as one and the same.

For the sake of this chapter, MHC is further defined as the practice of counseling *and* psychotherapy by persons formally trained, supervised, and credentialed. Depending on one's specialized training (e.g., psychiatry, psychiatric nursing), MHC also may include evaluating persons for and prescribing them psychotropic medications. Furthermore, the function of MHC is both salutary and remedial. This means that MHC is intended to promote not only coping, adaptive, and resilient behaviors as the expression of personal well-being, it also is intended to rectify, prevent, and/or alleviate distress and maladaptive behaviors.

Who Participates in Mental Health Counseling?

The question of who participates in mental health counseling (MHC) pertains to providers and recipients or consumers of MHC services. This section reviews the professionals who commonly provide MHC, as well as clients or patients of MHC, and those eligible for such services.

MHC Professionals

Identifying all of the mental health care professionals who provide MHC is not an easy task. In the MEPS survey mentioned earlier, a "mental health person/professional" is defined as "a person, such as a psychiatrist, psychologist, counselor, or social worker, trained to diagnose and treat emotional or mental health problems" (see http://meps.ahrq.gov). The National Alliance on Mental Illness (NAMI; Duckworth, 2013) expands this list by including psychiatric/mental health nurse practitioners, psychiatric/mental health nurses who are also clinical nurse specialists, and peer specialists. It is noteworthy that NAMI refers to "licensed professional counselors," a more specialized term, than the generic reference to "counselors."

How to distinguish among these professionals also is a challenge, not only for the public, but within professional groups as well. Pearlman (2013) characterized mental health care providers as comprising "widely varying and poorly understood scopes of practice of the various categories of mental health care professionals" (p. 330). In some of these professions the terminal degree to practice MHC is a doctoral degree (e.g., psychology, psychiatry). Other professions regard the master's degree as the terminal degree for MHC practice, including counseling and social work, although some aspects of social work can be conducted by persons without a graduate degree. These requirements are determined by accrediting bodies that set standards for academic training (e.g., Council for Accreditation of Counseling and Related Educational Programs) and regulatory boards (e.g., state licensure boards).

Sperry (2013) predicts that based on reimbursement trends (i.e., payment from third-parties, e.g., Medicaid/Medicare, private insurance companies), MHC will be conducted more by mental health counselors and social workers and less by psychologists. This is understandable given their numbers alone. The most recent biannual report of mental health statistics published by the Substance Abuse and Mental Health Services Administration (SAMHSA, 2012), *Mental Health, United States*, includes the number of mental health care providers by discipline or profession (pp. 158-159). Based on professional membership and credentialing (e.g., state licensure, professional certification), the number of social workers (baccalaureate level and graduate level combined; *N*=244,900) is almost twice that of counselors (graduate level only; *N*=128,886), who outnumber psychologists (graduate level only; *N*=92,227) by almost one-third. The fourth most populated mental health providers are marriage and family therapists (*N*=48,666), followed by psychiatrists (*N*=24,758) and advanced practice psychiatric nurses (*N*=9,742).

One group of mental health care providers not on the SAMHSA (2012) list (but on the NAMI list of providers mentioned earlier) is peer support providers (PSPs) or peer support specialists. Although not licensed as mental health care providers, PSPs represent an emerging behavioral health workforce (Salzer, Schwenk, & Brusilovskiy, 2010) "well suited to undertake the new tasks that will be required" in an increasingly integrated health care system (Manderscheid, in press, Staffing Implications for County and City Programs section, paragraph 2). That PSPs are a legitimate professional group is supported by their recognition by the Department of Health and Human Services as official mental health providers whose services can be reimbursed by Medicaid and Medicare (see State Medicaid Director Letter, 2007).

PSPs are "self-identified consumers who are in recovery from mental illness and/or substance use disorders" who must complete the training and certification as a PSP as defined by each state, and whose work must be (a) supervised by "a competent mental health professional" (defined by each state) and (b) incorporated into the routine comprehensive and individualized care planning services provided by a program of care (see State Medical Director Letter, 2007). A national survey (Salzer et al., 2010) of 291 employed/paid PSPs from 28 different states revealed that most of their time is spent at their employment site (as opposed to in the community, e.g., providing transportation) and that almost 50% of that time is spent providing individual services (as opposed to group services). The primary service provided by PSPs is peer support, defined as sharing personal experiences, providing mutual aid, and encouraging self-determination and personal responsibility.

Even in programs that do not include PSPs, distinguishing among other groups of mental health care providers remains challenging; this is likely to continue. Given the movement toward an increasingly more integrative health care system, predictions are that mental health care providers soon will be referred to as behavioral care professionals (BCPs; Cummings & Cummings, 2013) or behavioral health consultants (BHCs; Hunter, Goodie, Oordt, & Dobmeyer, 2009). Distinctions among them (e.g., based on graduate specialty training) will diminish and, as a group, BCPs and BHCs will be differentiated only from primary care physicians, who will be the providers to assume leadership for the delivery of mental health care. Indeed, "general practitioner or family doctor" was identified as the one group of professionals seen most often (58.5%) in the past year by persons with major depressive disorder (SAMHSA, 2013), next were those identified as "psychiatrist or psychotherapist" (34.4%), followed by "counselor" (24.6%), "psychologist" (24.3%), and "religious or spiritual advisor" (19%).

MHC Consumers and Eligible Recipients

Given the many different professionals involved in mental health counseling (MHC), who are the persons who participate (then and now) as MHC service recipients, consumers, or clients? Who are the persons who are eligible for such services (based on level of distress, mental illness) but who have *not* received services for a variety of reasons? That is, who are former, current, *and* prospective MHC clients?

The percentage of persons receiving any type of MHC (i.e., received mental health care from a general physician, psychiatrist, or other mental health care provider) has increased significantly since the early 1990s. Kessler et al. (2005a) compared 1990-1992 National Comorbidity Survey (NCS) data to 2001-2003 NCS Replication data and found that 20.1% of persons (ages 15 to 54 years) participating in these face-to-face household surveys reported receiving MHC in the previous 12 months in the early 2000s compared to only 12.2% in the early 1990s. Increased use was specific to general medical services and psychiatric services, but not to other mental health services. Using MEPS data (referred to earlier), Olfson and Marcus (2010) reported that the percentage of persons in the United States participating in outpatient psychotherapy (i.e., sought services from a mental health provider at least once) remained relatively unchanged in 1998 (3.37%) compared to 2007 (3.17%). The types of persons who made use of outpatient mental health services also did not change: more middle-age adults than children or older adults, more unmarried compared to married persons, more unemployed than employed persons, and more women than men. These demographics are somewhat similar to those found by Kessler et al. (2005a), with the addition of non-Hispanic Whites being more likely to use MHC than persons of other races. Among children and adolescents, more boys than girls have used mental health services in the past 3 months (Burns et al., 1995).

According to SAMHSA (2012), in 2009 approximately 20% of the adult U.S. population (or one in five adults) experienced some type of mental illness. However, only 13% of U.S. adults received some form of mental health service (e.g., inpatient, outpatient, prescription medication) in the past year. This disparity is referred to as unmet need, which increased dramatically from 4.3 million persons in 1997 to 7.2 million persons in 2011 (Roll, Kennedy, Tran, & Howell, 2013). This means that many more Americans with reported mental health needs are *not* receiving services than are, and this difference is more pronounced among the working-age population (ages 18-65) who are also of low income, unmarried persons, those without health insurance coverage (compared to those with private insurance) who are also in fair to poor health, and women (compared to men).

This unmet need seems to have increased even prior to 1997. Combining data from several national surveys, Vessey and Howard (1990) found that only 6-7% of persons who qualified for a mental health diagnosis would visit a mental health professional within 6 months. They also found that those who did make at least one visit to a mental health professional were likely to be middle-age highly educated White females who were either divorced or separated. This is not the exact same demographic profile; however, of those who *returned* for additional MHC sessions. Females were not more likely than males to return, and younger persons (18-20 year olds) were more likely to return. Being White, having a college degree, and having a higher income were demographics of those who returned to counseling.

Specific to the young adult population, Yu et al. (2008) investigated the MHC use of young adults (avg. age equal to 22) who had received MHC as adolescents. Compared to young adults *not* currently seeking MHC, those who *did* report participating in MHC in the past 12 months were significantly more likely to (a) be female (62%) than male (39%), (b) have received MHC in adolescence (24% vs. 12%), (c) currently attending school, and (d) receiving routine physical exams. An additional factor predicting greater use of MHC in this young adult population (compared to young adults not currently receiving MHC) was having a mother with a college or higher education. Overall, fewer young adults (7%) sought MHC than they had as adolescents (12%), and black and Asian young adults were less likely to seek MHC than White young adults.

Two factors that significantly increase eligibility for and use of MHC are being poor and having a chronic health condition. That poverty is associated with having a mental health condition is well established (U.S. DHHS, 1999). Using MEPS data, Vick, Jones, and Mitra (2012) found that those with severe psychiatric disorders experience some of the most extreme forms of poverty. Furthermore, the odds of being poor when at least one person in the household has a severe psychiatric disorder are three times the odds of other households being poor. This is especially true when the head of the household lacks a high school education and has been unemployed for at least one year. Burns et al.'s (1995) longitudinal study of mental health service use among children and adolescents in western North Carolina found that poverty was the greatest risk factor for a mental health diagnosis (20.3% of this sample qualified for a mental health diagnosis), most commonly anxiety and enuresis. In addition to poverty, physical health conditions are associated with mental health conditions and use of MHC. In one sample of persons with chronic health conditions (e.g., pain, cardiovascular disease) who were receiving medical care, 43% reported also recently receiving some form of mental health services (Ledoux, Barnett, Garcini, & Baker, 2009).

Where does Mental Health Counseling Take Place?

The settings of MHC have necessarily expanded in recent years to accommodate eligible consumers and to address unmet need and disparities (particularly for those of low SES and racial/ethnic minorities). Most mental health care is now provided in outpatient settings (SAMHSA, 2012) categorized by SAMHSA as either specialty settings (e.g., mental health facility, primary care setting, psychiatrist's office) or nonspecialty settings (e.g., schools, general physician offices, correctional facilities, emergency departments, nursing homes). The latter is characterized as "a key part of mental health treatment for adults in the United States" (SAMHSA, 2012, p. 22). Although current health care reform in the United States emphasizes primary care settings for MHC (reflecting an integrated system; see Alexander, Arnkoff, & Glass, 2013; Pearlman, 2013), nonspecialty settings are likely to expand. These include home-based care and care provided in other settings that are part of the client's natural environment, such as schools. Burns et al. (1995) identified the K-12 school setting as "the *de facto system* of care for children with mental health problems" (p. 152), given that 70-80% of children and adolescents who receive MHC (whether or not they meet criteria for a diagnosis) are seen by providers working in the school setting, mostly guidance counselors and school psychologists.

The increased use of MHC over the past 25 years has been prominent in settings providing general medical care (e.g., hospital emergency department, family doctor/primary care physician) and psychiatric services (whether inpatient or outpatient), reflecting a combination of specialty and nonspecialty settings. From the early 1990s to the early 2000s, Kessler et al. (2005a) noted substantial increases in the use of mental health services specific to general medical services (from 31.5% to 49.6%) and psychiatric services (from 19.6% to 25.8%), suggesting increases in pharmacological interventions. These increases compare to the slightly lower use in services when care was provided by other mental health care providers (from 43.5% to 41.9%) during this same period of time. These trends are likely to continue as MHC becomes more integrated into primary care.

The location of service provision does matter. Whereas once persons with mental health conditions were expected to travel to where the providers were located (e.g., to the often remote "insane asylums" of the 18th and 19th centuries), it has now become the expectation to literally meet persons where they are, that is, in their own natural living environment. Mobile crisis teams or ambulatory care services for persons with mental illness have been found to decrease hospitalization rates (Guo, Biegel, Johnsen, & Dyches, 2001; Scott, 2000) and to increase involvement in community-based mental health services within 90 days of a crisis, particularly for African Americans, those who are homeless, and those with severe mental illnesses (Dyches, Biegel, Johnsen, Guo, & Min, 2002). When it is law enforcement officers responding to crises, those officers with formal training in the Crisis Intervention Team (CIT) model (see Kasick & Bowling, 2013; Watson & Fulambarker, 2012) are less likely to respond with force (Compton et al., 2011) and more likely to direct persons with suspected mental health concerns to mental health care (Watson et al., 2010) than non-CIT trained police officers. Responding to mental health crises and providing *in vivo* care thus facilitates more immediate and less expensive care (i.e., decrease in hospitalization rates), targets those with unmet needs (e.g., the homeless, racial/ethnic minorities, those with severe mental illness), and seems to offer more humane and compassionate care (e.g., less force used). Mobile services such as the CIT model are consistent with evidence-based practices such as assertive community treatment (ACTx; DeLuca, Moser, & Bond, 2008) and multisystemic therapy (MST; Henggeler, 2001) that provide home-based care or services provided in the person's or family's natural environment and are conducted by a team of professionals.

Other *in vivo* forms of MHC include employee assistance programs (EAPs; e.g., services provided in the work environment) and services provided in the adult correctional and juvenile justice systems, child welfare system (particularly when children/adolescents have "serious emotional" disturbances; Burns et al., 1995), crisis care facilities (e.g., women's and homeless shelters), and nursing homes. Using data from the National Nursing Home Surveys (data from 1995, 1997, 1999, and 2004; commissioned by the Centers for Disease Control and Prevention), Li (2010) found that approximately 80% of facilities provided some form of mental health services to their residents, whether routinely (25%) or on-call (24%), or both (28%). No mention is made of the types of mental health services provided. Li also found that 22% of facilities (or 3,000) did not provide mental health services to its residents. Those that did not were more likely in smaller or rural facilities, facilities in regions other than the Northeast region of the United States, and facilities serving a small number of publicly insured residents.

More traditional settings for MHC are community-based mental health facilities and community-based drug and alcohol treatment facilities. Because it has been known for some time that co-occurring disorders (CODs; i.e., at least one mental health condition and at least one substance use disorder occurring at the same time, for the same person) are the rule rather than the exception whether persons are seen in mental health care settings or in substance use treatment settings (Brems & Johnson, 1997), integrated services for CODs (i.e., treating both at the same time) have become a standard of care (Rosenthal, 2013). This includes college and university counseling centers, which were one of the first settings of multidisciplinary practice (Kraft, 2008). The "high burden of mental health problems among college students" (Eisenberg, Hunt, & Speer, 2013, p. 64) and their increasing severity (Watkins, Hunt, & Eisenberg, 2011) are significant challenges for college/university counseling centers. To meet these needs, it will become increasingly important to train non-professionals (e.g., fellow students, staff, resident assistants, faculty) in recognizing mental health and substance use concerns among college students and referring students to appropriate care when necessary. This will involve educating a wide variety of persons on MHC so as to correct misperceptions and to diminish perceived stigma of MHC, stigma that is more pronounced among male than female students, undergraduates than graduates, and Asian-Pacific Islander and other non-White students, including international students (Golberstein, Eisenberg, & Gollust, 2008).

A Brief History of Mental Health Counseling

Compared to the practice of medicine, nursing, social work, and psychology, what is referred to today as *mental health counseling* (MHC) is relatively new. Even the word *counseling* has a very short history: its first known use is reported to be in 1927 (Merriam-Webster online dictionary). However, as stated earlier, the *practice* of counseling, as well as MHC, is not the domain of only one group of professionals. This also is true of psychotherapy, a practice that, in this chapter, is understood as the same as MHC. MHC thus is an interdisciplinary practice, a common practice regarded as a field rather than a profession. The historical review in this section is therefore shared by many mental health professions. Several recent works provide excellent chronicles of the history of mental health care in the United States. These include: Cautin (2011); Cutler, Sills, Svendsen, and Yeager (2013); DeLeon, Kenkel, Garcia-Shelton, and VandenBos (2011); Everett and Lee (2012); and Glosoff and Schwarz-Whittaker (2013). Readers are encouraged to consult these works for a more detailed history of mental health care in America; theseworks have informed this section.

The United States has a complicated and fascinating history of health care. Puritan and Judeo-Christian beliefs, ideals, and practices certainly influenced its development, and differences between moral care and medical care—as well as their unique combinations—continue today. MHC can be said to share the same history of what was and continues to be referred to as psychotherapy. Psychotherapy had as its beginnings moral treatments (e.g., humanistic care in supportive environments), mental healing (including spiritualism, early hypnosis, and pseudo-medical practices), and medical interventions (e.g., psychiatry, psychoanalysis). Humanistic care within a medical model that pursues innovation and undergoes perpetual reform describes a great deal of the practice of MHC today.

Early Reform

Moral treatment, including the mental hygiene movement, was regarded as an alternative to the typically harsh medical practices (or simply punishment) for persons who engaged in what was thought to be "deviant behavior," as well as for persons deemed "insane" with "disordered minds," referred to as "lunatics" or "maniacs" and relegated to institutional "asylums" for what often became the rest of their lives. The nonviolent and humane care for persons with mental illness was championed by such persons as Philippe Pinel in France (1745-1826), and Dorothea Dix (1802-1887) and Clifford Beers (1876-1943) in the United States. Their efforts to reform "the dark ages of mental health" (Everett & Lee, 2012, pp. 399-401) were met with skepticism, if not rebuke, and without a unifying theory or coalition it became evident that such humane practices were not viable on their own. To be effective, moral treatment needed to work in concert with the medical community. This was true particularly for personnel at state mental hospitals in the late 1880s providing care for persons with "mental and nervous diseases," practitioners who became some of the first psychiatric nurses (Stevens & Henrie, 1966).

Beginning in 1825, the number of regional- and state-run institutions for persons with mental illnesses grew exponentially. According to Everett and Lee (2012), this advancement is due in part to the debates over human rights violations associated with slavery taking place at the state and federal levels at that time. They explain (p. 401):

> Building a substantial asylum for persons with mental illnesses served as a civilized symbol of compassion and humanitarianism. Asylum construction provided ballast against the far more charged inhumanity and human rights issues associated with the abolition or continuation of slavery.

Treatment in these asylums comprised what was then regarded as medical interventions such as diet and rest cures, bloodletting, restraint, electricity, and hydrotherapy. Although not sounding very humanitarian today, these were hailed by the medical community as the only legitimate practices, separate from mental healing practices or the "mental therapeutics" that at that time were promoted by laypersons (e.g., clergy) and quasi-physicians (see Cautin, 2011, pp. 5-12). Medicine, however, underwent significant changes at the turn of the 20th century as a result of various scientific discoveries, such as germ theory. Just as certain diseases became increasingly associated with specific microorganisms, physicians began to entertain biological explanations for mental illness, as well as mental/cognitive explanations (e.g., unconscious, dissociation) for mental disorders and their treatment (e.g., suggestion, hypnosis, moral conviction). These latter explanations were also fueled by popular lay and religious movements at the time. As Cautin writes: "[I]n turn-of-the-century America, a psychotherapy movement was growing within the scientific community, stimulated by popular fascination and enthusiasm for mental therapeutics" (p. 6). Not only had science shifted the course of medicine; so, too, had non-scientific practices earlier branded as quackery. And as psychotherapy began to take shape as a legitimate practice, the medical profession was intent on claiming it as its own.

Psychotherapy and Professional Development

It was this early form of psychotherapy-as-medical-practice that welcomed Sigmund Freud's theory and practice of psychoanalysis. Psychoanalysis soon became a legitimate form of medical practice and the predominant form of psychotherapy for the next 30 to 40 years in the United States. Other forms of psychotherapy emerged prior to World War II, including behaviorism (led by J. B. Watson, 1878-1958) and Carl R. Rogers' (1902-1987) client/person-centered therapy. Although psychology was practiced alongside psychoanalysis in the early part of the 20th century (and mostly in academia and in scientific laboratories), it wasn't until World War II that psychology gained prominence. This was due to its use of intelligence testing (developed in the early 1900s and used during World War I to screen applicants for military service) and psychological testing, as well as the need for psychological intervention for war-related mental trauma. Psychotherapy was no longer "owned" by medicine or psychiatry; it now was becoming part of the scope of practice of other health care professionals as well.

As psychotherapy—and what also would be referred to as MHC—gained legitimacy and recognition, its reach extended to other professionals as well, not just psychiatrists or psychologists. These included psychiatric nurses, social workers, and professional counselors. This latter group includes in its history the practice of vocational guidance, a process and, what was believed then to be a scientific method, for helping someone decide on a calling or a vocation. This was important particularly for a developing nation: helping persons identify a field or occupation in which they could be successful made it possible for them to contribute to a growing society. Vocational guidance also was intended to prevent youth from drifting from one job to another so as to promote efficiency. In the late 1880s and into the early 1990s the freedom to choose for oneself a vocation was consistent with the climate of a developing nation influenced by immigrants (Glosoff & Schwarz-Whittaker, 2013). Pioneers and leaders in this movement were educators such as Lysander S. Richards (1835-1926), Frank Parsons (1854-1908), and Mr. Jesse B. Davis (1871-1955). They were the forerunners of today's career counselors and school counselors. It was also during this time (early 1900s) that MHC services began to be offered at college and universities, the first such program established at Princeton University in 1910 under the direction of a psychiatrist (Kraft, 2009).

Mental health care was shaped profoundly by World War II. Glosoff and Schwarz-Whittaker (2013, p. 38) refer to this time as "the confluence" of several mental health care movements and professions. Psychologists were not the only professionals to propagate in the 1940s. Vocational guidance personnel, rehabilitation counselors, and other counseling professionals also were sought by the U.S. military to help screen, assess, and assign personnel to various duties and to help soldiers with "battle neuroses." Cautin (2011) explains that "[t]he unprecedented need for mental health care among newly discharged veterans underscored the demand for more mental health professionals" (p. 24). The War Department established the Army Separation-Classification and Counseling Program in 1944 to address the vocational and emotional needs of returning soldiers, and the Veterans Administration (VA; established in 1930) instituted counseling centers in their hospitals (Glosoff & Schwarz-Whittaker). The National Mental Health Act was passed by the U.S. congress in 1946, which "signaled the federal government's commitment to prioritizing mental health" (Cautin, p. 26). This legislation provided funding for research into the prevention, diagnosis, and treatment of mental disorders, and in 1949 the National Institute of Mental Health (NIMH) was officially established.

Community-based Efforts

The next decade was no less eventful. The first edition of the *Diagnostic and Statistical Manual: Mental Disorders* was published by the American Psychiatric Association in 1952. The development of antipsychotic medications (e.g., chlorpromazine or Thorazine®; López-Muñoz et al., 2005) is in many ways responsible for the shift in mental health care from hospital settings to outpatient, community settings. The "psychopharmacological revolution" of the early and mid-1950s explains deinstitutionalization, although Cutler et al. (2013) cite the resurgence of "moral treatment" or "therapeutic communities" as an important contribution to the dramatic decrease in the patient population of state psychiatric hospitals, from 558,239 patients in 1955 to 71,619 in 1994 (Torrey, 1997, p. 8). It was also in the 1950s that the humanistic and nondirective therapeutic approach of Carl R. Rogers (1902-1987) gained prominence. His academic and clinical work began in the early 1940s with a focus on troubled youth. The National Defense Education Act (NDEA) of 1958 prioritized math and science education (in K-12, college, and graduate) to help prepare American youth to compete with their counterparts in the Soviet Union, which had launched the year before two Sputnik satellites. The NDEA also provided support for guidance counseling programs, bolstering the number of counseling professionals.

Subsequent federal legislation in the 1960s brought greater recognition to the practice of psychotherapy, expanding its relevance and reach beyond soldiers, war veterans, and the hospitalized mentally ill. The Community Mental Health Centers Act of 1963 established funding for the development of community-based mental health care programs. Passage of Medicare and Medicaid in the mid-1960s also "hastened the exodus of aged patients from hospitals to chronic nursing homes" (DeLeon et al., 2011, p. 41) and the beginnings of third-party insurance reimbursement plans (i.e., "managed care") in the 1970s set the stage for the integration of mental health care into general health care, an integration that only now is being realized. That MHC was not restricted to certain populations (e.g., very wealthy, severely mentally ill) or locations (e.g., psychiatric hospitals) was slowly becoming evident to the general population during this time. The number of mental health practitioners grew substantially and soo did the number of mental health problems and conditions, including substance use disorders. More educated persons sought out MHC and psychotherapy research increased considerably, especially with newer behavior therapies gaining prominence.

The attention given to mental health continued through the 1970s, with President Carter establishing the first President's Commission on Mental Health in 1977. This attention was short-lived, however. The Reagan administration's concern with lowering taxes and federal expenditures meant drastic cuts in federal support for mental health care in the 1980s. These cuts explained the proliferation of managed care plans by the late 1980s, plans that signaled increased regulation so as to contain costs. Managed care became standard operating procedure into the 1990s even as providers opposed its practice because of its negative effects on them (e.g., low morale) and on consumers (e.g., reduced access to care, limited services). The result, however, was the emergence of short-term and problem-focused therapies, as well as evidence-based practices. Psychiatrists began concentrating almost exclusively on pharmacological practice (due in large part to the growth in pharmacological treatments, e.g., anti-depressant medications), thus vacating their practice of psychotherapy (i.e., specifically "talk therapy") and opening doors for more non-medically trained professionals to practice psychotherapy (including master's-level practitioners, e.g., licensed counselors).

Recent Reform Efforts

It was at the end of the 1990s that U.S. Surgeon General Dr. David Satcher issued the first report on mental health by a U.S. Surgeon General. This report (U.S. DHHS, 1999) brought a needed spotlight on mental health and MHC as a legitimate form of health care. In a subsequent report (U.S. Department of Health and Human Services, 2001), Dr. Satcher brought further attention to existing ethnic and racial disparities in MHC, emphasizing that "culture counts."

This emphasis on mental health and MHC helped fuel the work of the New Freedom Commission on Mental Health (2003), an initiative of President George W. Bush. In its final report, the Commission outlined six goals of a transformed mental health system and 19 corresponding recommendations. One of the goals (Goal 1) is that Americans understand that mental health is essential to overall health, with a corresponding recommendation (1.2) that mental health be addressed with the same urgency as physical health. Another goal (Goal 2) is that mental health care is consumer and family driven, with a corresponding recommendation (2.1) to develop an individualized plan of care for every adult with a serious mental illness and child with a serious emotional disturbance. When the U.S. Congress passed the Mental Health Parity and Addiction Equity Act in 2008 (an extension of the 1996 Mental Health Parity Act), it seemed that the first of these six goals would soon be achieved. The Patient Protection and Affordable Care Act (PPACA), passed by the U.S. Congress in March 2010 during President Obama's first term in office (and aspects of which were upheld by the U.S. Supreme Court in October 2011), has almost guaranteed such equity. Not only has the PPACA legitimized mental health care; it has transformed health care. Implications are discussed in the next section.

Current Trends and Priorities in Mental Health Counseling

Even before passage of the Patient Protection and Affordable Care Act (PPACA), specific aspects of mental health (e.g., prevalence of suicide, co-occurring disorders) were demanding increased attention. To address these and other needs—and in response to scientific discoveries (e.g., expanding menu of psychotropic medications), policy initiatives at the state and federal levels (e.g., performance-based budgeting), the growth of consumer advocacy groups (e.g., NAMI), and the effects of U.S. military conflicts in Iraq and Afghanistan—the field of mental health care has necessarily changed. A few of these trends and priorities are mentioned here.

Integrated, Coordinated, Collaborative, and Comprehensive Care

Particularly over the past 10 to 15 years, there has been considerable interest in the integration of physical health care (or primary care) and mental health care (or behavioral health care) (see Blount, 1998; Cummings, Cummings, & Johnson, 1997; Cummings, O'Donohue, Hayes, & Follette, 2001; Hunter et al., 2009). What was then confined to mostly envisioning and experimenting with such a concept now has become a reality. This is a time of "transformation" in MHC (Yeager et al., 2013, p.5). The delivery of MHC essentially has changed and, in many ways, it is the PPPACA that is responsible for this. The PPACA requires that health care be delivered in an integrated fashion wherein all health care professionals (including primary care physicians and mental health care providers) work collaboratively so that care is coordinated and comprehensive. Mental health care providers now are expected to work with primary care physicians (PCPs) in a delivery system far different from the traditional 50-minute individual counseling session conducted on a weekly basis. The implications for service delivery and professional training in this new age are vast.

Although the PPACA was met with strong opposition and its initial implementation was fraught with miscalculations and other errors, Manderscheid (in press) regards the PPACA as "a wonderful opportunity to address many intractable behavioral health care problems in our communities" (Immediate Next Steps section, paragraph 2). Two aspects of the PPACA are Medicaid expansion and state health insurance exchanges, both of which, according to Manderscheid, promote equity in health insurance coverage and care access to reduce significant disparities that negatively affect persons of low socioeconomic status (SES) as well as racial/ethnic minorities. At the time of enrollment (projected to have begun January 1, 2014), it was predicted that 40% of persons benefitting from Medicaid expansion will have a behavioral health condition, and that 25% of persons in the state health insurance exchanges will have a behavioral health condition. Pearlman (2013) also noted the anticipated increase in the detection and provision of services for mental health conditions, especially for the previously uninsured, such as persons with severe and persistent mental illnesses (SPMI) who, she says, will represent a small but costly increase in mental health services. Mild to moderate forms of mental illness, she adds, will also demand increased services because they comprise the majority of mental illnesses and these conditions often go untreated. Mandersheid also anticipates that the eligible population to be served "will favor persons with primary substance use conditions" (Population and Service Implications for County and City Programs section, paragraph1). Features of the ACA that have significant implications specifically for persons with mental health conditions (and substance use disorders, or SUDs) are: (1) elimination of pre-existing condition exclusion; (2) family health insurance coverage for persons 26 years old or younger (a benefit given that many mental health conditions have onset in late adolescence/early adulthood, e.g., schizophrenia); (3) elimination of co-pay, deductible, and annual and lifetime limits for health insurance; and (4) insurance plan direct care expenditures (i.e., at least 80% of revenue of health insurance plans be directed to care delivery) (Manderscheid). There are essential health benefits (EHBs) in both the Medicaid expansion and state health insurance exchanges coverage plans for persons with SUDS and mental illness. These include outpatient, inpatient, and intensive outpatient treatment, crisis care, and prescription drug coverage, as recommended by the Coalition for Whole Health (a coalition formed to provide guidance and recommendations to policy makers prior to the PPACA; see http://www.coalitionforwholehealth.org/2012/01/ehb-consensus-principles-and-service-recommendations/).

In Medicaid expansion as part of PPACA, the integration of behavioral health and primary care will be addressed through a single entity, referred to as "Health Homes." This name is not to be understood as a location, but as a form or mechanism for providing holistic and integrated care. According to Manderscheid (in press), the main impetus for this form of care is to provide primary care to persons with behavioral health conditions who also suffer from chronic physical illnesses, and to provide mental health or behavioral health care to persons who also have health problems. For example, a person with schizophrenia will also receive services for his or her diabetes; and someone with a chronic heart condition will at the same time receive services for depression. These Health Homes will be coordinated by an Accountable Care Organization (ACO) and the ACO will be accountable for the health of the population (e.g., geographical region) it serves.

Two additional implications of integrative care that the PPACA has introduced are service financing and mental health workforce capacity. As set by the PPACA—and, indeed, what is anticipated for integrated health care in general—financing will no longer be by care or treatment episode, but by annual case, per person served. According to Manderscheid (in press), this type of financing system has "the potential to replace traditional approaches to managed care" (Performance Reform section, paragraph2). The workforce will change as well. As previously uninsured persons seek mental health services, "provider capacity will become an even more urgent concern" (Roll et al., 2013, p. 82). Pearlman (2013) anticipates a *decrease* in mental health care providers, based on the large influx of newly insured persons seeking mental health care. This decrease in providers will be seen particularly in "full-spectrum" providers. These are professionals who can provide not only "talk therapy" and diagnostic assessment and treatment, but also those who can prescribe psychotropic medications (e.g., psychiatrists, psychiatric/mental health nurse practitioners). Clearly, integrated health care—attributed in large part to the PPACA—has essentially redesigned MHC.

Co-occurring Disorders

It was mentioned earlier in this chapter that having a mental illness and a substance use disorder at the same time is a more common occurrence than having only one of these two conditions. This is understandable given that substance use disorders are the second most prevalent of the classes of disorders captured in the *Diagnostic and Statistical Manual of Mental Disorders*, fourth edition, text revision (*DSM-IV-TR*; American Psychiatric Association, 2000), the first being anxiety disorders and the third mood disorders (Rosenthal, 2013). From his review of recent prevalence research, Rosenthal reports that in the general U.S. population in a 12-month period, approximately 18% of persons who meet criteria for a substance use disorder also meet criteria for an anxiety disorder; this rate is approximately 20% for a mood disorder (e.g., major depression). Co-occurrence rates are highest when the substance use disorder is specifically a drug use disorder, such as cocaine or opioid dependence. In these cases, the co-occurrence rates are 23% for an anxiety disorder, 32% for a mood disorder, and 48% for a personality disorder (percentages rounded up). A diagnosis of antisocial personality disorder, in particular, dramatically increases the likelihood of a substance use disorder. For persons who seek either mental health or substance use treatment, the co-occurrence rates are quite high, anywhere from 30% to 70% (Rosenthal), and particularly for persons with severe and persistent mental illnesses such as schizophrenia (Mueser & Drake, 2007).

Sometimes referred to as dual disorders, concomitant or co-occurring disorders (CODs) also can include the presence of a medical condition, such as diabetes, HIV/AIDS, and hepatitis. This means that persons with CODs are challenged and burdened by many different stressors, including unemployment and poverty, unstable housing (including homelessness), involvement in the criminal justice system, and lack of family and other types of social support. The complex and chronic nature of CODs requires a treatment delivery system that is up to the task of providing comprehensive, compassionate, individualized, and integrated care. This implies that treatment providers are educated about CODs, can recognize previously undetected and neglected problems (e.g., family stress), and can provide a range of services (Mueser & Drake, 2007). This also means that persons with CODs should be able to enter the health care system at a range of community service sites, not just drug and alcohol treatment facilities, for example. This is the "no wrong door" policy of SAMHSA (2005).

Psychopharmacology

Several studies have noted a dramatic increase in the use of medications for mental health conditions over the past 15 years, an increase that has surpassed the use of psychotherapy not involving psychotropic medications (Fullerton, Busch, Normand, McGuire, & Epstein, 2011; Ledoux et al., 2009; Olfson & Marcus, 2010). This increase has taken place at the same time that rates of psychotherapy use have decreased, signifying that mental health care is increasingly equated with only using psychotropic medications, and less so with "talk therapy" (i.e., counseling or psychotherapy). In one study (Ledoux et al., 2009), 75% of patients frequenting a medical facility for various chronic conditions who reported also receiving mental health services stated that the mental health services they were receiving were psychotropic medications only. Another 20% of this sample reported receiving psychotherapy *and* psychotropic medications; and only 2% said they were receiving psychotherapy only as a mental health service. In another study of U.S. military veterans who completed an assessment in a VA hospital post-traumatic stress disorder (PTSD) program (Mott, Barrera, Hernandez, Graham, & Teng, 2014), 79% were referred for medication management, whereas only 39% were referred for individual counseling and 24% referred to group counseling. The increased use in only medication for mental health conditions is further illustrated in expenditures for this form of mental health care. For Medicaid enrollees in one state with a mental health condition, spending on psychotropic medications increased 110% from 1996 through 2005, with spending on antipsychotics (up 949%) accounting for most of this increase (Fullerton et al.).

The steep rise in the availability, referral for, expenditures, issued prescriptions, and use of medications for mental health conditions since at least 1987 in the United States (an increase not seen in other countries) is what Whitaker (2010) describes as "a modern plague" (the title of Chapter 1 of his book), one that he believes is actually "fueling the epidemic of disabling mental illness" in the United States today (p. 11). This is a rather unsettling pronouncement. It suggests that scientists, pharmaceutical companies, and prescribers of psychotropic medications (as well as those providers who encourage the use of prescribed medication among their clients) have a role in the increase in the number of Americans who have been identified over the past 25 to 30 years as having a mental illness. From Whitaker's critique of the pharmaceutical industry and the professionals who prescribe psychotropic medications, it seems that rather than promoting mental health, mental health care providers, in some ways, actually may be promoting mental illness. This *is* a very difficult "pill to swallow"! This suggestion will require candid and careful review by mental health care providers and the professional associations who represent them, especially as integrative health care becomes more established.

Expanded Service Settings

As mentioned earlier in this chapter, settings for service delivery have expanded greatly in the past 65 years. This is true more recently for primary care, in light of national health care reform that prioritizes the integration of MHC in primary care settings, such as hospitals and general physician offices, otherwise known as co-located care (Hunter et al., 2009). These settings may be more attractive to certain persons. Kaltman, de Mendoza, Gonzales, and Serrano (in press), for example, found that Latina immigrants preferred receiving MHC in primary care clinics because these are familiar places that offer a variety of health services at low cost.

Additional service settings are home-based care, correctional and other criminal justice settings, K-12 schools, and college/university campuses. Home-based care can be understood more broadly and inclusively as care provided in one's natural environment, otherwise known as *in vivo* care. This includes crisis intervention services and MHC provided in nursing homes, two of which were mentioned earlier. Although not a physical setting in the traditional sense, expanded service settings now include technology-based services such as computer-assisted programs that use multimedia and interactive features (e.g., use of smart phone technology). This use of technology is one of the six goals of a transformed mental health care system included in the final report of the New Freedom Commission on Mental Health (2003).

Advances in technology clearly hold promise for how psychotherapy is delivered. Because most persons with mental health concerns (including substance use problems) do not seek in-person treatment, technology-based services can address this unmet need, reaching a broad audience that has access to the Internet. The enthusiasm for using these types of services must be tempered however, because the quality and effectiveness of a myriad number of interventions within this category has yet to be established (Kiluk et al., 2011).

Affordable, Accessible, and Culturally Competent Care

One of the purposes of the Patient Protection and Affordable Care Act (PPACA) is to expand health insurance coverage to the approximately 32 million persons who lacked coverage at the time of the bill. This legislation is therefore intended to rectify the number one reason for not receiving mental health services in the past year among adults 18 years old and older who had a mental health need: could not afford the cost (SAMHSA, 2013). Forty-six percent identified this as the reason for not receiving care. This percentage is comparable to the 42% of young adults (average age of 22 years) in Yu et al.'s (2008) study who identified "couldn't pay" as the number one reason for not receiving MHC even though they reported having mental health needs. Cost was also the primary reason given by Latina immigrants for not seeking specialized mental health services, even though they were already receiving primary care services at a clinic serving low-income uninsured persons (Kaltman et al., in press). Because they thought MHC represented separate services, they thought MHC would require payment they did not have. This reinforces the need for integrated care as well as improved MHC marketing by health care professionals.

Other frequent reasons for not seeking MHC among adults who acknowledge having a mental health concern are: thinking the problem will go away, believing they can handle the problem without treatment, not having time, and not knowing where to go for services (SAMHSA, 2013; Yu et al., 2008). Lack of time and not knowing where or how to access services are accessibility issues, and these constitute another barrier to MHC. Other barriers include facilities that do not accommodate the needs of ethnic and racial minorities (e.g., not having on staff providers who speak the native or first language of persons in the community) and providers who are not skillful in culturally competent care (who may comprise the majority of practitioners; Sue & Sue, 2008). To make services more accessible, providers must invest in improving their own cross-cultural or multicultural counseling skills, made possible by culturally diverse immersion experiences and receiving supervision and other forms of feedback from cultural mentors. Furthermore, health care providers may need to invest more in home-based, *in vivo* services that, as mentioned earlier, are the thrust of many evidence-based practices (EBPs). These include cultural adaptations of EBPs.

Evidence-based Practices

Providing services that have demonstrated their effectiveness is clearly a priority in MHC and in health care in general. Evidence-based practices (EBPs) are approaches to care that have been empirically validated. This means they have proven their worth under careful and systematic scrutiny, and according to certain objective criteria. Findings from clinical research trials constitute one type of empirical validation or evidence. Others include clinician expertise and client input attesting to individualized and beneficial care.

The American Psychological Association (APA) has offered a useful definition of EBP, informed by evidence-based medicine: EBP is "the integration of the best available research with clinical expertise in the context of patient characteristics, culture, and preferences" (APA Presidential Task Force on Evidence-Based Practice, 2006, p. 273). A key word in this definition is *integration*, reinforcing the idea that EBP is not about technique or intervention (as is the case with empirically-supported treatments, or ESTs). It also is not about research only. Rather, EBP is a form or style of care that reflects the incorporation of good research, the skills of clinicians, and the responsiveness of system and providers to the unique characteristics of clients. In this way, EBP can be thought of as "both a philosophy and a set of problem-solving steps, using current best research evidence to make clinical decisions" (Mudford, McNeill, Walton, & Phillips, 2012, p. 5). The primary focus of EBP is thus on "empirically supported general content-domain practice elements" (Frueh, Ford, Elhai, & Grubaugh, 2012, p. 4), or "tried and true" psychotherapy operating procedures, such as cultivating and monitoring the therapeutic working alliance, routinely soliciting client feedback, and teaching clients skills to cope with specific symptoms. A common element in EBPs for children and adolescents is the reinforcement of appropriate behaviors, such as teaching new skills in the home and in the school setting, and motivating engagement in the counseling process

There are a number of organizations that maintain registries of EBPs, using different criteria to determine the designation of EBP. These include SAMHSA's National Registry of Evidence-based Programs and Practices (NREPP; www.nrepp.samhsa.gov), the APA's Society of Clinical Psychology (a division of APA; www.psychologicaltreatments.org), and the Cochrane Reviews (www.cochrane.org/cochrane-reviews). This latter registry is sponsored by the Cochrane Collaboration, a not-for-profit network of global health practitioners, researchers, and patient advocates who help interpret information from research to be of use to health care providers and recipients of care.

Sperry (2013) predicts that EBP will become the standard, with specific emphasis on motivational interviewing (Miller & Rollnick, 2013) and cognitive behavior therapy. Furthermore, provider-client collaboration (emphasized in many EBPs) will become more pronounced despite predictions that, in an integrated health care delivery system, the standard 50-minute therapeutic hour for outpatient psychotherapy will be reduced to 15- to 20-minute interactions that are highly focused (Hunter et al., 2009).

Suicide Assessment and Prevention

Although suicide assessment and prevention has always been a priority in health care, it has become an essential practice given recent trends. Suicide rates in the United States declined between 1986 and 1999, but annual rates increased by 0.7% from 1999 to 2005 (Hu, Wilcox, Wissow, & Baker, 2008). In each of these 7 years significant increases were noted among Whites (1.1% per year increase) in the 40-64 age range (2.7% per year increase for White men, and a 3.9% per year increase for White women), and in method (i.e., suicide by hanging/suffocation, a 4.9% per year increase, to 22%, surpassing poisoning at 18%). Over the 10-year period of 1992-2001, emergency department (ED) visits for suicide attempts almost doubled, from 0.8 to 1.5 visits per 1,000 visits, what Larkin, Smith, and Beautrais (2008) interpreted as nearly twice the rate of increase in mental health-related visits to EDs over the same time period. Specifically, suicide attempt ED visits increased significantly for non-Hispanic Whites, youth younger than 15 years, and adults in the 50-69 age range. Among adolescents, the prevalence of suicidal thinking increased slightly in 2010-2011, despite overall decreases noted in suicidal thinking in this age group from 1991-2011 (Lowry, Crosby, Brener, & Kann, 2014).

Recent military conflicts and national economic instability have contributed to increases in suicidality among the U.S. population. In 2001, suicide rates among military veterans receiving services in the VA were significantly higher than those in the general public, for men and women (McCarthy et al., 2009). This differential is also true for U.S. Army personnel, with Kuehn (2010) describing suicide among returning soldiers as an "epidemic." Furthermore, the economic recession that began in the United States in 2008 is associated with a 25% increase in suicides in the 2008-2010 time period (Reeves et al., 2012). This is a higher rate than in other countries also experiencing economic hardship during this same time.

These recent increases in suicidal thinking, attempts, and completions noted among segments of the adult and adolescent population in the United States require health care professionals to remain vigilant and responsive. This is true in light of Yu et al.'s finding (2008) that a relatively low percentage of young adults reported accessing MHC in the past year to address mild to severe depressive symptoms (15%), suicidal ideation (23%), one suicide attempt (41%), or multiple suicide attempts (38%), despite their report of depression and suicidal ideation/attempts in the past 12 months. Larkin et al. (2008) attributed the increase in ED visits for suicide attempts during the decade of 1992-2001 in part to "a coincident increase in publicity, destigmatization, and normalization of both suicide attempts and help-seeking behavior" (p. 77). However, they added that an increase in substance abuse by both men and women might also explain the increase. This is consistent with Kuehn's (2010) report that alcohol and/or drug use was involved in almost one-third of completed suicides and 45% of attempted suicides in the U.S. Army between 2003 and 2009.

Granello (2013) provides additional and more detailed statistics on the current magnitude of suicidality, including its economic costs and the number of family and community members who are affected by someone's attempted or completed suicide. She also reviews an earlier version of what is now the U.S. DHHS's (2012) *2012 National Strategy for Suicide Prevention*, a collaborative of the U.S. Surgeon General and the National Action Alliance for Suicide Prevention (see http://www.surgeongeneral.gov/library/reports/national-strategy-suicide-prevention/full_report-rev.pdf). The current document lists goals and objectives associated with four strategic directions to address suicide risk in the

U.S. population (e.g., create supportive environments to promote the population's general health and reduce the risk for suicidal behaviors and related problems).

Target Populations and Concerns in Mental Health Counseling

In addition to the trends and priorities in mental health counseling (MHC) discussed in the previous section are target populations and related concerns that warrant special consideration. These include specific age groups, racial/ethnic and other cultural groups (e.g., lesbian, gay, bisexual, and transgender, or LGBT, persons), socioeconomic considerations, crisis and trauma, veterans of the U.S. armed forces, and stigma.

Age Groups

For MHC to be relevant, accessible, and effective, it must be configured to different age groups. This means that services are developed, selected, and adapted based on the age of current and prospective clients. Configuration thus involves such things as the setting of care, developmental challenges and milestones (e.g., puberty, social or peer status, individuation, fertility and childbirth, menopause, retirement), the persons involved in care (e.g., parents, teachers, adult children), formats of care (e.g., individual or group counseling), and methods of delivery (e.g., computer- or technology-based, animal-assisted therapy, outdoor and adventure-based therapy). For children and adolescents, for example, services must be provided at school. This is a natural environment for persons in this age group. One of the recommendations of the New Freedom Commission on Mental Health (2003) was to improve and expand school mental health programs. This was specific to fulfilling Goal 4 of a transformed mental health system: early mental health screening, assessment, and referral to services are common practice. Continued efforts toward this goal are essential because the majority of children and adolescents with mental health problems are *not* receiving professional help for those problems. In the Burns et al. (1995) mentioned previously, only 40% of children and adolescents with severe mental health conditions had received care in the previous 3 months.

Access to MHC for older teenagers and young adolescents is crucial given that substance use, onset of substance use problems, and onset of symptoms associated with certain mental health problems (e.g., schizophrenia) take place during this developmental period. University administrators in one study (Watkins et al., 2011) reported an increase in the severity of mental health issues among students at their universities. College and university counseling centers must be equipped to address these and other age-specific concerns, doing so in a manner that engages young persons, rather than inadvertently dismisses them. For example, it may not be realistic to recommend abstinence from substance use or sexual activity to persons in this age group. Rather, credible and feasible safety or harm reduction strategies are taught instead, such as remaining with a group of friends for the entire night when going off-campus, not drinking alcohol given to you by a stranger, and sending prepared text alerts to trusted friends when needed.

Older age groups face a variety of challenges that are and can be the focus of MHC. These include child-rearing, locating and retaining employment, accessing entitlements (e.g., Medicare, Social Security), grief and bereavement, physical illness (e.g., heart disease, diabetes), and caring for elderly parents. Proactive and accessible MHC for this age group is provided in hospital and emergency care settings, community centers, private practice clinics, churches and other religious worship settings, and the workplace (e.g., employee assistance programs). As with a younger age population, mental health care provider collaboration is essential for this age group, such as coordinating MHC with a person's primary care physician.

Racial, Ethnic, and Other Cultural Groups

In the Preface of his 2001 report on *Mental Health: Culture, Race, and Ethnicity*, former U.S. Surgeon General Dr. David Satcher declared succinctly, "culture counts" (U.S. DHHS, 2001). This truth is much more robust today, due in part to the significant increases in ethnic and racial groups in the United States. According to the U.S. Census Bureau (Humes, Jones, & Ramirez, 2011), persons of Hispanic/Latino ethnicity increased by 43% from 2000 to 2010, representing more than half of the growth in the total U.S. population during the two most recent census periods. In terms of race, non-White persons had the least population increase (5.7%). The highest increase in racial groups was among persons identifying as Asian (43.3%), followed by Native Hawaiian and Other Pacific Islander (35.4%), persons identifying as being of two or more races (32%) or of some other race (24.4%), American Indian and Alaska Native (18.4%), and Black or African American (12.3%). Although Whites comprise the majority of the population in the United States today (72.4%), their representation decreased since the 2000 census (from 75.1%), the only racial group to do so. And projections are that all minority groups combined, now 37% of the population, will comprise 57% of the population in 2060 (see www.census.gov/newsroom/releases/archives/population/cb12-243.html).

That "culture counts" is not just due to population size, however. Culture counts because of the values people hold, values that are influenced by their cultural backgrounds and identity, or mixture of cultural identities. Values also are influenced by past and current positions of power—whether privileged with access to a wide range of resources and self-determination capabilities that protect against certain hardships or disenfranchised from sources of support and advancement, prevented from exercising certain societal or civil rights (e.g., legally marry same-sex partner). Persons who have experienced forms of oppression and discrimination are likely to have different values from those who have been inoculated from such violations and have maintained societal decision-making powers. Values are expressed in behavior and therefore signify the essence, or at least the uniqueness, of an individual. Valuing the uniqueness of a person by understanding his or her cultural background and identity is at the heart of MHC. Cultural background and identity extends beyond race and ethnicity to include such influences as sexual orientation and gender identity/expression, religious affiliation and spiritual beliefs/practices, ability/disability status, age, educational attainment, and socioeconomic status (SES)—all of which have varying degrees of power and privilege.

Persons who have (a) limited access to positions of societal power and privilege and (b) experienced forms of discrimination and oppression *because of* their cultural backgrounds and identities are persons who merit priority mental health care. Such persons are likely to be in poorer health and less likely to improve without health care intervention than those persons who have resources, societal decision-making power, and have not experienced discrimination because of their cultural background and identity. For example, using MEPS data, Chen and Rizzo (2010) found that during the decade of 1996 to 2006, Whites were significantly more likely to have participated in MHC than Latinos, but not significantly more likely than African Americans to do so. However, Latinos and African Americans were more likely than Caucasians to (a) report worse mental health status and general health status, (b) be uninsured, and (c) be enrolled in Medicaid. In addition, English-speaking persons were more likely to receive MHC than non-English-speaking persons. In a study of Asian and Latino sexual minority adults (using data from the 2002-2003 National Latino and Asian American Study), Chae and Ayala (2010) found that adopting an identity as lesbian, gay, or bisexual (LGB)—also known as "coming out"—was associated with *higher* levels of psychological distress than *not* adopting such an identity. They attributed these levels of distress to such things as rejection by family members, social isolation, and experiences of sexuality discrimination, experiences not shared by non-LGB Latino and Asian persons (or non-LGB persons in general). These and other findings underscore the importance of designing MHC to effectively address the needs of culturally diverse clientele.

Socioeconomic Considerations

Socioeconomic status (SES) refers to the position of individuals, families, and households based on the factors of education, income, and wealth (Martins et al., 2012). National household surveys have determined that having a mental illness—specifically a serious mental illness (Kessler et al., 2008; Vick et al., 2012)—is associated with low earnings, and thus low SES (Martins et al., 2012). Illnesses associated with low income and SES include bipolar disorder, schizophrenia, major depressive disorder, substance use disorders, and any illness accompanied with a recent suicide attempt that had a serious lethality intent. And, as mentioned earlier in this chapter, poverty is not only associated with having a serious mental illness; it also is associated with living in the same household with at least one person who has a serious mental illness (Vick et al.), as might be the circumstance of children whose parent or other adult caregiver is struggling with a mental illness.

Crisis and Trauma

Crisis can be understood as an unexpected and unwelcome, even tragic, event or circumstance that requires immediate attention and response. Crises can be large-scale events affecting many people at the same time, such as natural disasters (e.g., hurricanes, mudslides, tornadoes) or human-made disasters (e.g., terrorist attack, school shooting, city water contamination); or they can be more person-specific, the result of personal predicaments such as the death of a loved one, divorce, or terminal illness (Storr, Azur, Bass, & Wilcox, 2012). Because crises can and often are traumatic (referred to as traumatic events), the word *trauma* is often used interchangeably with that of *crisis*. But trauma also can be thought of as the response to a crisis or one way that a crisis is experienced. In this sense exposure to a crisis can produce trauma, and trauma is thus the result or residue of such exposure.

In general, trauma encompasses emotionally overwhelming experiences that can have devastating effects psychologically, physically, and societally. Estimates are that at least 50% of the U.S. population will experience one traumatic event in their lifetimes (Storr et al.). Individual traumatic events include exposure to violence, involvement in accidents and experiencing acute injury, developing certain illnesses (e.g., life-threatening), involvement in military combat and exposure to war-time stress, and civilian exposure to war (e.g., refugee status). Experiencing any one or more of these events can be complex (as in repeated exposure to violence) and chronic, developing into PTSD. In one national sample (McLaughlin et al., 2013), a majority (61.8%) of 13- to 17-year olds reported experiencing at least one potentially traumatic event in their lifetime. These events were defined as experiencing first-hand interpersonal violence (e.g., physical abuse by a care giver), accidents (e.g., automobile accident, natural or human-made disaster), injuries, and the unexpected death of a loved one, or witnessing the death or serious injury of another.

Although a focus on trauma has existed for quite some time, it was only with the addition of PTSD as a diagnosis in the third edition of the *DSM* (*DSM-III*; American Psychiatric Association, 1980) that trauma assumed clinical priority (Storr et al., 2012). PTSD is an anxiety disorder and anxiety disorders are now considered the most prevalent class of disorders in the United States, with approximately 7% of American adults meeting criteria for PTSD (Kessler et al., 2005b). In addition to its diagnostic prevalence, the considerable attention given to trauma in recent years can be attributed in part to greater journalistic and social media coverage of global crises (e.g., natural disasters), military intervention and combat (and the effect on soldiers as well as citizens, e.g., immigrants and refugees), and domestic acts of violence (e.g., kidnapping, rape) and other forms of aggressive behavior (e.g., bullying). Increased awareness of various forms of crises and its traumatic effects also can be attributed to increasing ethnic and racial diversity in the United States and advances made in civil rights (e.g., legalization of same-sex marriages in 17 U.S. states and the District of Columbia) that forces acknowledgement of and public dialogue about various forms of cultural trauma (e.g., current and historical oppression and discrimination). As a result, trauma-focused care, crisis response (e.g., psychological first aid and debriefing), and disaster services have become specialty areas in the mental health field.

Veterans

In 2011, there were approximately 21.6 million U.S. armed services veterans, the vast majority of whom were men (92.5%) in the 55- to 74-year-old age range (46%; National Center for Veterans Analysis and Statistics, 2013). Although the overall veteran population is predicted to decrease by almost 8 million by the year 2040, the percent of female veterans, minority veterans, and those who served during the Gulf War era is projected to increase rather substantially by 2040 (see http://www.va.gov/VETDATA/Quick_Facts.asp). This means that health care services, including MHC, will be needed for an increasingly diverse veteran population.

It is encouraging that in one study (Rosen et al., 2011), the vast majority of veterans (88%) reported wanting help for emotional or mental health problems and 81% of them initiated counseling in VA-sponsored programs (e.g., VA outpatient clinic, VA Veterans Center mostly staffed by veterans) after receiving a diagnosis of PTSD. One-third of these veterans participated in 8 or more counseling sessions within one year of receiving the diagnosis of PTSD and, in another study (DeViva, in press), 75% of veterans who completed PTSD-specific care received 9 or more counseling sessions, half of them completing treatment within 15 weeks.

It remains a concern however, that a significant number of veterans do not receive the mental health care that they need. For example, in DeViva's (in press) study, 38% of veterans (specifically of the conflicts in Iraq and Afghanistan) seen in a primary care VA facility over a 2.5-year period in one region of the United States who were referred to specialty PTSD services within the VA did not follow-up on the referral. Furthermore, only 12% of the veterans who followed-up on these referrals completed treatment, and 43% were closed after being seen at least once and then discontinuing treatment and not responding to follow-up calls to reengage in services. Of the veterans who never started or completed the PTSD care they were referred to, 47% did not have any other encounter with a mental health provider in the VA system, 38% met with a medication provider at least once but received no psychotherapy, and only 15% engaged in other (non-PTSD) VA mental health services.

The setting of initial care may make a difference in rates of follow-through for veterans with mental health needs. For example, veterans diagnosed with PTSD in a medical setting versus a mental health setting were *less* likely to initiate counseling, and those who had concerns about fitting in at a VA center for counseling were more likely to be women (Rosen et al., 2011). Stigma was cited as a reason *not* to seek help for personal concerns by 35% of these veterans, and veterans who participated in 8 or more counseling sessions at an outpatient VA medical center reported *greater* rather than less stigma concerns, leading Rosen et al. to surmise that "feeling bad about requiring help may be a potential adverse effect of treatment rather than a barrier to care" (p. 883). Both seem to be true and necessitate a consideration of stigma.

Stigma

The stigma of having a mental health condition and seeking MHC is a concern of all target populations. The New Freedom Commission on Mental Health (2003) defined stigma as "a cluster of negative attitudes and beliefs that motivate the general public to fear, reject, avoid, and discriminate against people with mental illnesses" (p. 7). As such, stigma represents a significant barrier to MHC. Negative or prejudicial views of mental health and MHC held by society (e.g., mental illness is a sign of weakness or immorality) and by individuals (e.g., persons who are coerced into unpleasant and invasive treatment) explain why many persons who need MHC do not obtain it. Five reasons given by adults (at least 18 years of age) for *not* seeking MHC in the past year, even though they recognized a need for some type of MHC, appear to be associated with stigma (SAMHSA, 2013): concern about confidentiality (9.6%), might cause neighbors or community to have a negative opinion (9.5%), fear of being committed/having to take medicine (9.5%), did not want others to find out (8.2%), and might have negative effect on job (8.1%).

Corrigan (2004) describes stigma toward persons with mental illness according to four social-cognitive processes: (1) cues (e.g., physical appearance, psychiatric symptoms, labels), (2) stereotypes or categorical information about persons with mental illness (e.g., "They are not able to hold a job" or "They are dangerous") that not everyone agrees with, (3) prejudice or negative stereotypes of persons with mental illness that can generate negative emotional reactions (e.g., "They all scare me!"), and (4) discrimination, defined as the behavioral response to prejudicial stereotypes (e.g., avoidance, not employing or hiring someone solely because of a known or suspected mental illness). Corrigan further distinguishes between public stigma and self-stigma. *Public stigma* refers to the prejudicial and discriminatory actions taken by a naïve public toward persons with mental illness. These can include the policies of private and governmental institutions that discriminate against persons with mental illness, otherwise known as structural stigma (Corrigan, Markowitz, & Watson, 2004). *Self-stigma* comprises actions taken by someone with mental illness because he or she has endorsed and internalized public stigma. These behaviors include not taking prescribed medication, not continuing in needed treatment, or engaging in self-destructive behavior, such as deliberate self-injury. Stigma might also be expressed toward family members of a person with mental illness. *Associative stigma* or *courtesy stigma* refers to prejudice and discriminatory behaviors shown to family members simply because they are related to someone with a mental illness (Phelan, Bromet, & Link, 1998).

These forms of stigma explain to a considerable degree the educational, employment, and health care disparities that persons with mental illness experience (Cummings, Lucas, & Druss, 2013). This includes accessing and remaining in needed mental health care. For example, some of the Latina immigrants with histories of trauma who were interviewed by Kaltman et al. (in press) believed that consulting a mental health specialist or simply considering a consultation with a mental health specialist was the equivalent of being or becoming "crazy." Although educating adults and adolescents about mental illness is effective in diminishing their stigma toward persons with mental illness, face-to-face contact with persons with mental illness is more effective. Corrigan, Morris, Michaels, Rafacz, and Rüsch (2012) explain this primary finding of their meta-analysis of 72 research studies in this way: "Meeting people with serious mental illness seems to do more to challenge stigma than educationally contrasting myths versus facts of mental illness" (p. 969).

Key Practices and Formats in Mental Health Counseling

No one source can provide an exhaustive list of the important practices in mental health counseling (MHC). This chapter is by far no exception. Given the breadth of mental health care professions and providers (e.g., counselors, psychiatric nurse practitioners), as well as current and prospective service recipients, a compendium of MHC practices may in fact be impossible. What are presented in this section are prominent and common practices in MHC, irrespective of profession. These practices have been selected in part because they have been found in counseling and psychotherapy research over a number of years to improve quality of care and client outcomes.

Marketing and Promoting Mental Health Counseling to the Public

One practice many mental health practitioners may not consider is marketing mental health counseling (MHC) to the general public. This can be thought of as enlightening an audience beyond one's current clientele about the purpose, process, and benefits of MHC. Professional associations and consumer advocacy groups (e.g., NAMI) do this on a regular basis by, for example, sponsoring public service announcements and fundraising events (e.g., the Walk to End Alzheimer's, sponsored by the Alzheimer's Association). Individual practitioners however, can inform local communities about MHC, doing so not simply to "drum up business" for their own facility or private practice, but to promote mental health and wellbeing. One of the standards in the American Counseling Association's *ACA Code of Ethics* (2014) is that counselors contribute to the public good by providing services with little or no financial gain (Standard C.6.E.). These contributions may include speaking to groups (e.g., Rotary Club, local clergy/ministerial association) and sharing professional information (e.g., educating police officers about the signs and symptoms of certain mental illnesses). Engaging in this form of public education can dispel myths about mental illness and its treatment, thereby helping to diminish stigma.

Correcting the misperceptions of MHC as portrayed in the media is an important first step in marketing MHC. Butler and Hyler (2005) identified five myths of child and adolescent mental illness portrayed in Hollywood films, one of them being the myth that a child with what is described as a "mental illness" can be cured with enough love. This and other myths have the deleterious effects of not only "feed[ing] hopes that parents' children might be otherwise gifted, but...also feed[ing] fears that parents are to blame, that psychiatrists will usurp their parental role, and that the profession itself is a sham (p. 520). Specific to addiction treatment, Kosovski and Smith (2011, p. 853) determined that one popular TV show, *Intervention*, conveys "contradictory and misleading messages" about addiction and family functioning and "grossly exaggerates and misrepresents both treatment approaches and outcomes." They stated that the "exaggerated narratives" featured on this show "have the potential to do harm" (p. 857) by (1) fostering a false sense of optimism about the success of family-based interventions and the availability of desired treatments, and (2) influencing viewers with substance use problems to not get treatment because their experiences of addiction may not be consistent with the experiences of addiction among family members on the show.

A second step is describing exactly what takes place in MHC. Kaltman et al. (in press) found that the most salient barrier to accessing mental health services among Latina immigrants, separate from cost, was uncertainty about what seeking care would entail, not knowing what to expect from treatment. The researchers interpreted this finding as reinforcing the need for psychoeducation "to increase mental health literacy and improve treatment acceptability" (p. 8). And when descriptions of MHC are positive, apprehensions about MHC involvement are likely to lessen. For example, compared to reading a neutral description of a counseling interaction, college students without a history of MHC who read a positive description of a counseling interaction were more likely to report a reduction in fear and stigma about MHC, particularly for male college students (Ægisdóttir, O'Heron, Hartong, Haynes, & Linville, 2011).

Corrigan (2011) outlines five principles for social marketing campaigns to reduce stigma about mental illness. These principles also can be followed by individual practitioners to improve what Kaltman et al. (in press) described as mental health literacy and openness to MHC mentioned earlier. Although not presented below in the following sequence, the principles can be remembered easily by the acronym TLC3: targeted, local, credible, continuous contact.

First among these principles is that the general public must have face-to-face *contact* with persons with mental illness. Practitioners can ask former clients who are maintaining gains made in MHC to accompany them to a local civic group to provide their testimonials of recovery. This is to be done however, only with thoughtful and careful preparation. Former clients may comprise those now practicing as peer support specialists, the paraprofessional group mentioned earlier in this chapter. Second, the audience members must comprise a *targeted* group, such as local business owners who are potential employers of persons with mental illness. A targeted audience also suggests the third principle of marketing campaigns, that they are geared to a *local* community, including its ethnic and racial composition, and resources already available (e.g., VA hospital or center nearby). Fourth, efforts to reduce stigma must be *credible*. For example, persons providing their testimony must be believable and represent persons to which the targeted audience can relate (e.g., look like me or a loved one). The fifth and final principle of stigma-reducing practices is that contact with persons who are in recovery from mental illness and/or addiction must be *continuous*. Hearing the story of only one person and one time only is insufficient to enhance mental health literacy within a particular community over time. As Corrigan explains: multiple and varying messages to different target audiences over time remind mental health practitioners that "stigma change is not easily accomplished and requires ongoing efforts and continuous quality assessment of those efforts" (p. 826).

Identifying and Inviting Prospective Service Recipients

Just as stigma-reducing campaigns must target a specific audience, so too must mental health practitioners target their services to specific client populations, persons eligible for and who would benefit from MHC. In an integrated care model, this means that mental health providers will need to increasingly collaborate with medical professionals to promote the use of mental health services among persons with medical and mental health conditions. The physician's or other medical provider's referral for mental health care is key. This is exemplified in Ledoux et al.'s (2009) study. They found that among persons with chronic medical conditions and mental health concerns (e.g., depression), the strongest predictor of recent mental health care use was being referred to mental health services by a healthcare provider. The second strongest predictor was the person's perceived need for these services.

Based on their findings, Ledoux et al. (2009) offered two recommendations: (1) provide opportunities for medical patients to be exposed to mental health care providers, so that medical patients develop a better understanding of how MHC can be beneficial; and (2) improve medical care providers' (e.g., physicians) knowledge of early symptoms of mental health conditions so as to reduce the amount of time between the onset of symptoms and initiating MHC. These practices may be more feasible as mental health care providers establish and maintain good working relationships with physicians in their local community.

Engagement as Style and Strategy

Engaging clients in treatment is a key practice in several EBPs, including motivational interviewing (MI) and assertive community treatment (ACTx). It also is a primary outcome in many clinical trials of treatment efficacy. Although engagement has not been clearly defined separate from or in addition to attendance, numerous studies indicate that persons who enter most forms of MHC (e.g., addiction treatment, home-based or *in vivo* services) and remain actively involved in their care improve considerably more than persons who do not enter MHC, discontinue after a short period of time (sometimes known as premature termination or "drop out"), or assume a passive role in their care (what some might describe as "going through the motions"). Sometimes referred to as client persistence or retention, specific client behaviors that exemplify engagement are such things as understanding treatment, rating the therapeutic relationship as strong, completing tasks outside of therapy that were agreed upon with the clinician, being committed to care, and continued attendance.

What is it exactly that counselors or therapists can do to encourage client engagement? How do practitioners join with clients to promote client investment and participation in MHC? In MI, this clinician engagement style and strategy is what is known as the "spirit" of MI (Miller & Rollnick, 2013): the MI clinician is compassionate, collaborative, evocative, and accepting. In other words, because the clinician's priority is the client's wellbeing, the counselor partners with the client's expertise by eliciting the client's own reasons for and ideas about change (using many empathic reflections to affirm and reinforce the client's own language about change), doing so in a way that supports the client's own autonomy or self-determination. This clinician style has been found to reduce client resistance or, more accurately, therapeutic discord, and to increase client consideration of change and participation in change behaviors (e.g., decreasing or abstaining from alcohol consumption). Because 38% of U.S. military veterans never followed-up on the PTSD-specific treatment they were referred to at the VA, DeViva (in press) recommends developing "motivation-enhancing interventions that can be administered in primary or secondary health care settings" (p. 5), interventions that are consistent with the style of MI.

The word *assertive* in the name of ACTx refers to the style and strategy of client engagement. Specifically, ACTx team members are proactive in enlisting client engagement, going to where persons with needs are, rather than expecting them to travel to where professionals are located. ACTx is a longstanding EBP developed in the early 1970s to reduce psychiatric hospitalizations and support independent living in the community for persons with severe and persistent mental illnesses, such as schizophrenia (see Schmidt, Pinninti, Garfinkle, & Solomon, 2013). ACTx providers thus interact with and provide assistance to potential clients and already enlisted consumers in their own natural living environments, that is, they provide *in vivo* care. Initial interactions with eligible recipients may occur in homeless shelters, on city streets, in fast-food restaurants, under bridges, or in homeless tent communities. A recent study (Manuel et al., 2013) of 34 ACTx teams in New York City (representing 239 team members), found that the two most common interventions used by ACTx members to engage eligible persons in treatment were positive inducements (e.g., buying lunch or cigarettes to help build a relationship) and verbal guidance (e.g., reminding consumers to do/not to do certain things).

Overall, an engaging counselor style is one that is welcoming, validating, and collaborative—not just at the beginning of care, but throughout the care process. Strategies associated with this style, though, are important particularly at the outset. For example, program directors of four mental health facilities in New York City reported a 70-80% first-session attendance rate (and a two-thirds attendance rate for 6 or more counseling sessions) when one or more strategies were implemented specifically to promote attendance (Smith et al., 2010). These strategies included making phone calls prior to the scheduled session, not simply to remind the person of the appointment, but more importantly to address potential barriers to attendance (e.g., transportation, child care); having the same provider who conducted the initial clinical interview serve as the client's ongoing provider so as to reduce the number of new staff clients encounter; and developing a "contract for services" clearly stating the rights and responsibilities of the client (e.g., keeping appointments, participating in goal setting) as well as the provider (e.g., meet with client at scheduled times, treat client with respect and as a partner in the process of change).

Comprehensive Assessment

Conducting a comprehensive assessment typically is the first formal or official task for mental health care providers when they meet with a newly assigned client. It also is known as the clinical interview or intake and essentially is an information-gathering session intended to obtain baseline information about client functioning (current and by history) so as to determine a preliminary diagnosis and treatment plan. In addition to clarifying the client's reason for visit, taking inventory of concerns and needs, and assessing the severity of presenting symptoms, the assessment process also should include learning of client strengths, resources, culture, and preferences. This is crucial for client engagement. Lindsey et al. (in press) defined assessment as the "measurement of client's strengths/needs through a variety of methods (e.g., interviews, questionnaires, observations, or record reviews) during which the therapist can engage clients through building rapport and an alliance" (Table 2). Defined in this way, Lindsey et al. found that assessment was one of the best practices to engage children and their caregivers in treatment, based on their review of research on the common elements of treatment engagement in children's mental health.

Because it is often the first in-person meeting between the client and a mental health care provider, the assessment sets the tone for the type of care the client can expect to receive. First impressions matter! There is no guarantee that clients will return for a subsequent visit. Indeed, there is research to suggest that up to one-third of clients do not return for a second psychotherapy visit (Simon, Imel, Ludman, & Steinfeld, 2012). To promote client engagement with male college students without a history of MHC, Ægisdóttir et al. (2010)

recommended discussing fears and common negative attitudes about MHC in the first session. In substance abuse counseling, Miller and Carroll (2006, p. 309) recommended that providers keep questions "to the absolutely necessary minimum" during assessment so that new clients can "tell their story and express their concerns and goals." Asking too many questions—especially at the outset—can prevent treatment from being welcoming and attractive. Because of the high rates of co-occurrence, this recommendation pertains to MHC as well.

During the assessment, the mental health provider often follows an interview protocol, asking the client—and perhaps family members in attendance, too—questions pertaining to current symptoms and history of concerns in the areas of mental health, substance use, medical status, legal involvement, physical or psychological abuse or trauma, family dynamics and social supports, education, religious affiliation/spirituality, and other areas that assist in clarifying the client's reason for visit and treatment needs. Depending on the mental health provider (e.g., psychiatrist) or assessment setting (e.g., specialized addiction treatment center), the assessment may include further testing, such as urinalysis. For psychologists, the assessment can consume a considerable amount of time. Norcross and Rogan (2013) found that approximately 36% of psychologists' overall time spent in practice was devoted to tasks performed during the assessment: standardized testing of personality (11% of overall time); assessment of interests, symptoms, and intelligence/cognitive functioning (10% of overall time); and diagnostic assessment (11% of overall time). Some psychologists also might conduct neuropsychological testing during the assessment.

Soliciting and Responding to Client Feedback

Given the amount of information clients are asked to provide during the assessment, and given the importance of client engagement, it is imperative that mental health providers routinely solicit and respond to client feedback. This can be as simple as asking periodically: "How is this going for you right now?" or "What has been helpful and not so helpful thus far?" For client responses to these questions to be taken seriously, counselors must allow time for the client to respond and then to process responses with the client, doing so in the style of engagement (e.g., adopting the "spirit" of MI).

Several EBPs have as a standard practice the collection of client feedback at different times during the therapy process. In multisystemic therapy (MST), for example, parents or other care providers of adolescents are asked to evaluate their family's therapist using a standard measure. Measures developed specifically to garner client feedback (e.g., preferences, satisfaction, current level of distress) that can be used in different counseling approaches include the Outcome Questionnaire (OQ; www.oqmeasures.com) and the Outcome and Session Rating Scale (see http://scottdmiller.com). These two measures are intended to be used routinely (e.g., at the beginning of each individual counseling session) for the purpose of monitoring client progress. Based on client feedback, providers can modify their approach, as needed, to better match client needs and preferences. This practice is part of what is known as patient- or client-focused research (see Lambert, 2010), which has demonstrated that clients improve when their providers make "course corrections" (e.g., more frequent sessions) in response to client feedback (e.g., lack of client progress, as indicated by deteriorating scores on the OQ, for example). This is true not only for individual clients but also for couples (Anker, Duncan, & Sparks, 2009).

Orientation, Preparation, and Further Engagement

Whether it occurs before or after assessment, providing clients with an orientation to MHC contributes to their treatment engagement and progress. Orientation is also known as preparatory education and it explains the purpose and process of MHC, as well as clarifies the roles and responsibilities of clients and providers. This can be done in a one-on-one conversation between client and counselor, discussed during the first session of group counseling, or presented in video format for all new clients to view in the waiting room or in a separate room. This latter method however, was found not to influence attendance rates or outcome of therapy at one clinic, perhaps because it was not interactive (i.e., passive format), viewed as impersonal, and that the majority (67%) of clients had participated in therapy previously (Strassle, Borckardt, Handler, & Nash, 2011). To be effective, therefore, any orientation procedure must be current and tailored to the treatment setting, as well as to the individual provider (e.g., explaining philosophy of care). It also should describe how MHC can be helpful. From a focus group of 38 low-income African American perinatal women with depression, not viewing MHC as effective was one of the reasons for not seeking MHC (Leis et al., 2011). One woman explained it this way (p. 317):

> It [psychotherapy] don't work. It don't change the situation. They push treatment, because they say you talk about it you feel better. The problem is tell me how to get over the problem or tell me how to fix the problem, don't just sit there and get paid to listen to me talk to you. That's not helping me.

To engage each new client in MHC and to reduce early or premature departure from the counseling process, Swift, Greenberg, Whipple, and Kominiak (2012) recommend that orientation include the following seven elements: (a) education about realistic expectations about duration of MHC and recovery or patterns of change, (b) role induction (i.e., explanation of roles and responsibilities of client and provider so that client knows what will be expected of him/her and what to expect from provider), (c) accommodating client preferences (e.g., providing advice only at client invitation), (d) strengthening early hope, (f) fostering the therapeutic alliance or partnership (e.g., ensuring agreement on goals and tasks before proceeding with certain interventions), and (g) assessing and discussing treatment progress (i.e., routinely soliciting feedback from client about perceptions of care and progress made).

Education

A common practice in MHC is to provide education to help clients and their families better understand and make sense of their presenting concerns, symptoms (and corresponding diagnosis), and ways to improve their current functioning and to feel better. This not only is part of the orientation process (i.e., informing clients about what they can expect in MHC), it is also a critical component of several counseling approaches. Skills training, for example, is a key practice in behavior therapy and CBT. Skills that are taught using these methods can include decision-making, parenting (e.g., discipline), assertiveness, effective communication, healthy and mindful eating, emotion regulation (e.g., managing anger), and relapse prevention. In DBT (an integration of CBT and the Eastern philosophy of acceptance), for example, four categories of core skills are taught in individual and group therapy sessions: mindfulness, interpersonal effectiveness, emotion regulation, and distress tolerance. Specific mindfulness skills include in-the-moment observation of or focused attention on internal processes (e.g., breathing) and external events (e.g., using visual and auditory senses to notice current surroundings). Although it is one of four core skills, mindfulness is a skill that is fundamental to the three other skills. Interpersonal effectiveness skills emphasize healthy communication methods (e.g., assertiveness) and emotion regulation skills include being able to recognize and name current emotions. Distress tolerance skills include avoiding stressful stimuli by engaging in distracting activities, as well as accepting or coming face-to-face with painful memories.

As with all interventions in MHC, education and skills training should be specific to the needs and preferences of each client or client system (e.g., family unit). They should not be delivered *en masse* as if to an unknown or vague audience. This means, for example, learning first about the client's English proficiency and language preference, reading ability, cultural views and values (e.g., time orientation, respect for elders, family composition, mental health care providers as authority figures), and preferred learning style (e.g., reading handouts, watching videos, interacting in a group setting). And, as discussed earlier, a key practice in MHC involves routinely soliciting and then responding to client feedback, altering the counseling methods used as needed. In MI, education or any form of information-giving is supplied only after securing client permission.

For skills training and other types of educational interventions to be effective, consistent application of the information or skills is necessary. This means that education and training are not about simply gaining more knowledge or becoming more aware of something. Rather, they are about behavior change. Applied or experiential education and skills training in MHC therefore involves practicing new behaviors. An important point to make here is that counselors need to model target skills before they can expect clients to demonstrate them. This sequence is often missed by many practitioners. When teaching assertiveness skills, for example, the counselor will first verbalize and also "act out" being assertive to a person in the client's life by standing up and making eye contact with the client in session, and then communicating emotion and wishes in a calm and steady voice. Obtaining client feedback and processing the counselor's modeling of assertiveness is important before having the client try out assertive behavior. Doing so ensures that the client understands the target behavior or skill and that the subsequent role play or behavior rehearsal is realistic.

One method used in skills training is that of technology and multimedia. Nunes et al. (2010) describe several technology-based programs and interventions specifically designed for children and adolescents. These include the use of (a) animation in software programs to engage children and teenagers with autism spectrum disorders in specific skills training (e.g., recognizing emotions in others, developing social problem-solving skills), (b) multimedia for youth with social skill deficits (e.g., developing videos of target behaviors, including video self-modeling), (c) anonymous response and online polling software (e.g., clickers) for group participants to share perspectives, and (d) handheld devices to track mood and behaviors in real-time outside of counseling. Nunes et al. advise however, that technology is merely a tool for mental health providers to use in appropriate and creative ways to enhance MHC.

MHC Formats

The format of MHC typically refers to the number and type of persons included in at least one person's care. These comprise *individual*, *group*, *couples*, and *family* formats, or modes. Format of care is therefore distinguished from setting and modality, the latter referring to how care is delivered (e.g., interventions used, counseling approach or method implemented, including pharmacotherapy), which sometimes can be irrespective of format. The format used often depends on the treatment setting (e.g., inpatient, outpatient, in-home or *in vivo*), the presenting concern, the sex and age of the identified client (as well as other cultural aspects), and the approach or modality endorsed by the provider and/or the setting, as well as the provider's discipline. For example, group counseling is the predominant format used in substance abuse treatment facilities in the United States, couples and family formats often are used by providers who subscribe to systemic theories and who are credentialed as marriage and family therapists, a family format (or the involvement of at least one parent or adult care giver) is considered standard when the identified client is a minor or an older adult, and individual counseling is the primary format for most practitioners in private practice. In a recent survey of psychologists (Norcross & Rogan, 2013), individual counseling or psychotherapy was found to be the most common format used. Among those who worked, on average, 40 hours per week, they reported 80% of their time was devoted to individual work.

Although the formats used may be dictated by the setting (and resources available) and provider preferences and discipline, it is important to supply formats that match the needs and preferences of the identified client. For example, in general, individual counseling is preferred by women, particularly those with substance use disorders (McCrady, Epstein, Cook, Jensen, & Ladd, 2011), Latina immigrants with a history of trauma and experiencing symptoms of depression (Kaltman, in press), and low-income women with perceived mental health concerns who, in Nadeem, Lange, and Miranda's (2008) sample, were primarily Black and Hispanic women. Honoring their preferences may determine the progress they make in counseling. For example, in one study (Ryan, Nitsun, Gilbert, & Mason, 2005), although slightly more women with a history of childhood sexual abuse chose individual counseling rather than group counseling, those who chose group counseling made improvements during and after treatment at comparable rates to those women who chose and participated in individual counseling.

Because of their young age, children and teenagers do not always have a choice about having adult family members involved in their care. Some states (e.g., California, Illinois) allow minors who are at least 12 years of age to consent to mental health treatment or counseling services for a maximum number of sessions without parental consent or involvement. However, it is the standard that when children and adolescents are the identified clients, MHC will necessarily involve their adult care givers. This does not mean however, that family counseling will be conducted at each session. It means that adult family members will be consulted and will attend at least some of the counseling sessions. This is a standard also applicable to identified clients who are older adults, although the family members who may be involved are spouses/life partners and/or children.

Family and Other Collateral Consultation

Periodically consulting with family members or other persons in the client's life (known collectively as collaterals) is a key practice in MHC regardless of the client's age. Of course this is done only with client permission, following state laws and professional codes of ethics. Collaterals can provide another perspective to help clarify MHC goals. They also can serve to support client efforts toward change, perhaps with coaching from the mental health care provider (e.g., "Notice the times when he's *not* fighting and reward him with praise at the end of the day"). In this way collaterals can serve as an ally to the client as well as to the mental health care provider, although the identified client remains the provider's priority.

Consultation with family members and other collaterals (e.g., friend, roommate, coach), including referral source (e.g., family caseworker, probation officer) can take place in person or over the telephone, whether or not client is present. Procedures for consultation need to be negotiated with the client and clarified with the collateral prior to consultation. Calling a family member while the client is present (e.g., conference call using speaker phone) may be the preferred method in certain case. Feedback from collaterals can also be obtained by postal mail (e.g., parent completing a family questionnaire, with responses shared and processed with client) or by email (following guidelines for the electronic transmission of confidential material). Again, the purpose and procedures of any consultation need to be clarified and understood in advance.

Individualized Care

Regardless of format and who or if other persons in the client's life are consulted, clients need and deserve individualized care. This means, among other things, that services are tailored or customized to their specific needs, preferences, and culture. (Recall that attending to these client factors is an element of evidence-based practice, based on the APA definition provided earlier in the chapter.) For child and adolescent clients for example, a key strategy in any EBP is to reinforce client behaviors that indicate movement toward target behaviors. Individualized care implies that treatment or care plans are flexible and modified according to changes in client circumstance. It also implies that attention has been given to cultivating and maintaining a strong therapeutic alliance or client-counselor connection, a factor that accounts for up to 30% of client improvement in MHC (Lambert, 1992).

With the advent of integrated behavioral health care (i.e., MHC in primary care settings), the frequency of client-provider interactions—or at least the extent to which clients will have contact with aspects of MHC—is likely to increase. Alexander et al. (2010) attribute this increase to the use of technology platforms. They anticipate that interventions such as phone consultation (e.g., already used in DBT), text messaging, and computer- and Internet-based interventions will be delivered more frequently than they are currently. More frequent and real-time contact with MHC will make it much more possible to individualize care.

Professional Consultation and Treatment Teams

The advent of integrated health care necessitates professional consultation and collaboration. No longer can professionals work independently, without routinely consulting their peers. Consultation includes engaging in regular clinical and/or administrative supervision and periodic peer supervision. Whether conducted individually or as a group, professional consultation and supervision promotes accountability, stimulates critical thinking and complex case conceptualization, allows for proper ethical decision-making, and contributes to provider professional development and well-being. At least two studies have identified the lasting beneficial effects of supervision on clinicians (Lucock, Hall, & Noble, 2006; Orlinksy et al., 2001), with one study (Knudsen, Ducharme, & Roman, 2008) reporting that receiving or participating in clinical supervision was associated with less emotional exhaustion and less turnover intention compared to those not receiving clinical supervision.

Mental health services provided by a multidisciplinary treatment team already has become the standard of care in many settings (e.g., community-based mental health). This is true for several of the evidence-based practices (EBPs) already mentioned in this chapter: dialectical behavior therapy, multisystemic therapy, and assertive community treatment (ACTx; DeLuca et al., 2008). Davis and Biltz (1998) defined a multidisciplinary team as "a community of professionals, some from different professional backgrounds, who are bound by common mission, goals, and expected outcomes. They work with a shared population of patients within the same physical space" (p. 242).

Specific to ACTx, the treatment team is comprised of, at minimum, a psychiatrist, nurse, mental health therapist or clinician, and a case manager (Schmidt et al., 2013). Many teams also include a peer support specialist, described earlier in this chapter. Consumers also are members of the treatment team, with Schmidt et al. describing them as "perhaps the most important members of the team, not only because they are the focus of assessment and treatment, but also because, without their active collaboration, ACTx services will be ineffective" (p. 295). It is the team and not an individual that provides services to consumers. ACTx team members thus share responsibility for all tasks and consumers on the team's caseload, and the team meets daily to ensure that all are informed of the status of all consumers engaged in care. Most teams have 10 to 12 members and the standard staff-to-consumer ratio is one to 10-12, with a maximum of 120 consumers served by one ACTx team.

There is considerable evidence to support ACTx's benefit to consumers, including reduced hospitalization stays, engagement in ongoing care, reducing symptoms, obtaining housing, and improving their quality of life (Rosen, Mueser, & Teesson, 2007). Furthermore, ACTx has been found to protect staff members from burnout (Boyer & Bond, 1999), owing, it seems, to the team approach of ACTx. The ACTx approach exemplifies behavioral health integration, fulfilling the three conditions of integration that Strosahl (2001) outlined: (1) services and providers are co-located, meaning that not only are providers operating in the same physical location, but they also are working together on the same treatment team and sharing the same clients or patients; (2) the full spectrum of behavioral health needs of a primary care population are addressed, medical and behavioral; and (3) integration is based on and guided by a philosophy or mission of true integration so that behavioral health is not a specialty service, but a routine part of medical or primary care.

Medication Management

The dramatic increase in the use of pharmacological services in the past 15 years was mentioned earlier in this chapter. In integrated behavioral health care, the use of psychotropic medications (e.g., for symptoms of anxiety, depression) will continue, becoming a standard part of MHC. Although not all mental health care providers are qualified to evaluate persons for medication or to prescribe and dispense medications, all providers generally work with clients who are taking psychotropic medications or who would benefit from doing so. This means that all providers have a part in medication management. For non-medical practitioners, this includes discussing with clients the costs and benefits of medication adherence, listening to and then processing with clients their concerns about stigma and medication side-effects. Given that psychiatry today is less so about psychotherapy and primarily about evaluating and prescribing medications, and that psychiatric consultation sessions are often delayed (i.e., wait time of 3-6 months to get in) and then are extremely brief (e.g., 10-15 minutes), clients often are not able to express any concerns fully or to raise questions directly with the prescribing physician (see Carlat, 2010).

To make MHC more accessible and responsive to persons with mental health conditions, non-medical providers will need to play a more prominent role in medication management. This means consulting routinely with medical providers (e.g., nurses, physicians), taking time to understand and process concerns about medication use with clients during individual counseling sessions, and marketing MHC as not just about pharmacology. This latter practice will be helpful particularly for those with unmet needs (discussed earlier in this chapter). In the one study (Leis et al., 2011) of low-income African American perinatal women described earlier, for example, their primary perception of MHC was that it is limited to medication dispensation, thus preventing their willingness to seek out MHC if they were feeling depressed. They also thought that the MHC provider would rush to make a diagnosis without taking time to understand their problem or concerns. Efforts to alter perceptions such as these so as to rectify at least one barrier to care will become increasingly important for all mental health care providers.

Facilitating Referrals

In MHC, referrals are understood as recommendations or mandates given to a person to receive general or specific forms of care. Persons also refer themselves to MHC (known as self-referrals). The practice of referring persons to initial, specialized, more intensive or higher-level, and different formats and settings of care is common among mental health care providers. Primary care physicians and psychiatrists, for example, refer patients to counseling and psychotherapy; and non-medical mental health care providers refer ongoing clients to medical providers (e.g., for a physical exam, medication evaluation)—this latter type of referral occurring more often than the former. Clients seen in individual MHC are referred to group counseling or to couples or family counseling formats; patients being discharged from a hospital setting are referred to outpatient MHC; and students in a K-12 school setting are referred to the school counselor for individual counseling or to the school psychologist for certain types of testing.

Despite its common practice, relatively little is known about how to facilitate a referral. Key in this wording is that referrals are *facilitated* or carefully managed and not simply "doled out." Because of high caseloads and limited time, it can be easy or tempting for providers to make referrals hastily, as if in passing. Their wording also may be imperative (e.g., "should" or "must"), the recommended service described vaguely, and time may not be devoted to explaining the provider's recommendation or to processing it fully with clients and their family.

For referrals to be effective (i.e., clients follow-through on the referral and access the recommended service), the provider's recommendation must be explained, the recommended service described and clarified (i.e., exactly what is being referred), the client's need for the recommended care and his or her readiness to follow-through assessed, the meaning and implications of the referral explored (e.g., cost, discontinuing current care or adding on to it?), options provided (e.g., more than one group available, starting now vs. waiting), sufficient time allotted to process the referral, and a plan negotiated. It also is helpful when the referring provider follow-ups with the client to inquire about accessing the recommended care. For example, a majority (58%) of college students seen in one university counseling center followed-through on a referral to obtain off-campus therapy (Owen, Devdas, & Rodolfa, 2007). Their primary reasons for doing so were that they believed they needed the recommended care, they were motivated to follow through, and their counselor at the university counseling center followed-up with them after the referral. Those who did not follow-through with the referral cited cost as the primary reason. One concern in this study is that a majority of the students who did not follow-through with the off-campus referral were students of color. This suggests that MHC offered in accessible and familiar surroundings (e.g., on-campus counseling center) may be preferable for persons for whom stigma of mental health may be a concern.

Continued Care

Continued care is more than following-through on referrals given. It means continuing to provide needed services in a familiar and welcoming environment. For persons with chronic conditions (e.g., autism spectrum disorder, severe and persistent mental illnesses), ongoing care is essential. Some might refer to continued care as aftercare or maintenance, particularly if it is subsequent to an intensive form of care (e.g., inpatient treatment). In this sense, the purpose of continued care is to maintain or to support client stability and to prevent relapse (e.g., need to return to hospital).

Continued care also can be likened to intermittent care, meaning that MHC is available and accessed at different points in a person's life, when it is needed. One indication that MHC has been successful is when clients report an openness and willingness to participate in MHC in the future, as needed. A good policy for any mental health care provider is to "leave the light on" and to "keep the door ajar" for recently discharged clients. This does not mean fostering client dependency on a provider; rather, it means that the client leaves MHC knowing that assistance at a later time, in another setting, and with another provider is available and will be helpful if current supports (e.g., skills learned in MHC) are not sufficient to manage future challenges.

Ethical and Legal Considerations in Mental Health Counseling

A comprehensive discussion of ethical and legal considerations in mental health counseling (MHC) is beyond the scope of this chapter. It is vitally important however, to include a section that highlights the fundamental ethical and legal considerations in MHC. Readers are encouraged to consult in-depth works on ethical and legal issues in MHC. Among these are Corey, Corey, Corey, and Callanan (2015); Pope and Vasquez (2011); Remley and Herlihy (2014); and Welfel (2013).

The vast majority of mental health care providers are licensed professionals whose practice is recognized by state law and regulated by a state licensing board. The primary purpose of each state's licensing board is to protect the citizens of the state from the unethical and/or illegal actions of licensed professionals. The one group of professionals mentioned earlier in the chapter, whose practice does not seem to be governed by any state law (i.e., they are not licensed), are peer support providers or specialists. State certification for these paraprofessionals is available (e.g., Wisconsin, Illinois) however, signifying completion of formal training, and there is a professional association, now known as the International Association of Peer Supporters (http://inaops.org). Its stated purpose is to promote the inclusion of peer support specialists in mental health systems around the world.

There are professional associations for all other mental health care providers, such as the American Counseling Association (ACA; see www.counseling.org) for professional counselors and counseling students. These associations represent the interest of members of the profession and all have developed ethical guidelines for members of the profession to follow. Indeed, that there is a code of conduct or ethics is one of the characteristics that defines a profession. A code of ethics is a collection of standards of practice, each standard specifying behaviors expected and becoming of a member of that profession. Ethical standards are derived from (a) the values of a profession (e.g., honoring human diversity and embracing a multicultural approach); (b) basic moral values and behaviors (e.g., regarding human life as sacred), as well as personal moral values (e.g., integrity, humility); and (c) principles that guide ethical conduct and decision-making. Most professional codes of ethics share the same five or six ethical principles. The six principles in the *ACA Code of Ethics* (2014) are: *autonomy* (promote another person's right to decision-making and self-regulation), *nonmaleficence* (do no harm), *beneficence* (do good, or promote another person's wellbeing), *justice* (treat persons equally and fairly), *fidelity* (remain true to your word, following through on professional commitments), and *veracity* (deal truthfully with others). These principles form the foundation of ethical decision-making and behavior.

That the practice of all mental health care providers is, for the most part, governed by state law and regulated by a state agency (by virtue of needing to be licensed), and also spelled out in professional codes of ethics, signifies the serious business of MHC. It certainly is not to be entered into lightly. All mental health care providers work with persons who are often in a state of distress and vulnerability. The wellbeing of clients thus must be prioritized and their care safeguarded. Regulations and other standards of practice—such as are in state law and professional codes of ethics—are therefore essential.

Confidentiality

Chief among the standards of ethical practice is confidentiality, the respect of a client's right to privacy. Honoring confidentiality also is a legal practice, written into state and federal laws. No form of MHC can proceed or continue without this assurance. Indeed, when low-income African American perinatal women were asked their reasons for not seeing a mental health care provider if they were depressed, many cited concerns about confidentiality (Leis et al., 2011). Several said that the provider might relay the content of counseling conversations to Child Protective Services, for example, thus jeopardizing their custody of their children.

Upholding confidentiality means that information pertaining to a client is not disclosed by practitioners without the client's written consent. The content of this information includes, but is not limited to, the client's identity, his or her disclosures in MHC, and the practitioner's assessment and treatment recommendations. Forms of communication in which the client's information must be protected are such things as verbal disclosures (e.g., conversations among treatment providers), print materials (e.g., written psychotherapy notes), and electronic/digital communication (e.g., email, audio recordings). It is critical that clients understand the limits to confidentiality. Some of these are when the client threatens to kill him- or herself or someone else, the provider becomes suspicious of child or elder abuse or neglect (whether client is involved as victim or perpetrator), and a court of law issues a court order for client records.

Informed Consent

Client understanding of confidentiality and its limits is part of the informed consent process. Free consent or agreement to participate and continue in MHC is the client's right (consistent with the ethical principle of autonomy), and disclosure of relevant information so that the client is able to make a decision free of coercion is the mental health care provider's responsibility (Welfel, 2013). This is an ongoing process, not simply one task completed at the beginning of MHC. The client has the right to be informed of the risks and benefits of all interventions that are recommended during the course of treatment and certainly before any is implemented. Proceeding with any new plan of action occurs only after the client agrees. For children and youth (and others who are in the care of an adult legal custodian), the clinician seeks their assent. This means that minors—and others whose comprehension and capacity to choose are limited—remain involved in the decision-making process and express their understanding so that consenting adults are not the only ones making decisions for them.

Duty to Warn

There are occasions when client consent is not necessary for the mental health care provider to breach confidentiality. These are when the safety and life of the client or another person are in danger. Again, these constitute exceptions to confidentiality and must be understood by the client before and during MHC. The duty to warn is a legal mandate in some states (e.g., California, Ohio) when a client has made an explicit threat to enact violence at any moment against another identifiable person or group of people. The duty is the clinician's and involves alerting authorities (e.g., campus police) to the client's clearly expressed intent. The clinician also may need to notify other persons (e.g., potential victims) to protect their safety. Taking action is carefully thought through and other professionals are consulted in the process.

Supervision

In most mental health care professions, students and those new to the profession (e.g., recently licensed) are required to receive supervision by a qualified practitioner. This is both an ethical standard and a legal mandate.

The purpose of supervision is to protect the welfare of clients seen by the student or new professional, as well as to promote the supervisee's professional development. Because a provider's learning and development continue throughout his or her career (or should), some professional groups (e.g., British Association for Counselling and Psychotherapy, BACP) regard supervision as an ongoing practice, continuing even after residency or independent licensure. Indeed, in its *Ethical Framework*, the BACP (2013) requires its members to receive regular and ongoing formal supervision, citing supervision as an obligation to enhance the quality of services offered to clients, thus fulfilling the ethical principle of beneficence (see www.bacp.co.uk).

The continuous practice of supervision is essential for learning new skills (e.g., those associated with EBPs) and has been described as "best practice" by program directors of mental health agencies in New York City (Smith et al., 2010). Specifically, program directors claimed that supervision retains effective staff (i.e., minimize staff turnover), promotes staff wellbeing and morale, and enhances staff productivity. As mentioned earlier, Knudsen et al. (2008) found that clinical supervision was associated with less emotional exhaustion and lower turnover intention among 823 substance abuse treatment providers from 109 treatment settings. These findings lend support to the growing evidence-base of clinical supervision (see Milne, 2009).

Cultural Competence

Receiving supervision is essential particularly in gaining cultural competence, now an ethical standard. The *ACA Code of Ethics* (2014) defines "multicultural/diversity competence" as a counselor's "cultural and diversity awareness and knowledge about self and others, and how this awareness and knowledge are applied effectively in practice with clients and client groups" ("Glossary of Terms," p. 20). It is demonstrated, for example, in communicating the purpose and limits of confidentiality to clients (see "Introduction" to Section B: *Confidentiality and Privacy* of the *ACA Code of Ethics*, 2014) and in working with specific cultural groups (e.g., racial/ethnic minorities, LGBT persons; see Section C.2.: *Professional Competence*).

Two important points need to be made about cultural competence: it is a demonstrable skill and, as with all skills, it requires constant practice and honing. First, becoming aware of and learning about diverse persons are not sufficient indicators of cultural competence. It is the *demonstration* of awareness and knowledge that is the observable skill. The primary measure of competence thus is in *how* a mental health care provider speaks of and communicates with diverse clients and their families. This means, for example, not speaking of diverse clients as "them" or even as "others" (i.e., separate from a particular standard), and it also means not regarding diverse clients as defective or deficient in some way, thereby needing to be enlightened, "rescued," or "restored" to a certain status.

Second, to a large extent, the skill of cultural competence is the outgrowth of the clinician's own awareness of his or her own cultural identity (or identities), values, stereotypes, and biases, which are all learned and shaped from interacting with diverse clients. As a result, old ideas and practices may be shed, and new perspectives formed that are then expressed in new and more skillful behaviors. This is what makes cultural competence an ongoing challenge, a process, and not a destination to which one can ever "finally arrive." The same is true for empathy. And one of the benefits of continuous supervision is to be able to wrestle with and to work through the challenges of cultural competence with an array of clients—as well as at different times in one's own life and career—and doing so under the guidance of another mental health care provider (i.e., supervisor). The feedback, correction, and support of a supervisor are vital in furthering cultural competence.

Mental Health Care Provider Self-care

That the practice of MHC is challenging cannot be emphasized enough. Challenges include conveying empathy to clients who have been violent and remain unremorseful, learning the details of a young client's exposure to repeated trauma, learning that a long-time client committed suicide, working in a facility with high productivity requirements (e.g., meeting face-to-face with outpatient clients for at least 24 billable clock hours in a 40-hour work week) and limited supervision, and working through one's prejudicial views of certain groups of persons, views that are prominent in one's family of origin. As mentioned earlier, this is not a profession to be entered into lightly. It is not for the faint of heart. Rather, this work requires stamina and resilience.

Because of the challenges inherent in MHC, mental health care providers must engage in self-care practices. Indeed, this is an ethical standard and, according to one professional association, it is an ethical principle. The *ACA Code of Ethics* (2014) regards self-care as a professional responsibility, its purpose "to maintain and promote [counselors'] own emotional, physical, mental, and spiritual well-being to best meet their professional responsibilities" ("Introduction" to Section 2: *Professional Responsibility*). In its *Ethical*

Framework, the BACP (see www.bacp.co.uk) lists *self-respect* as one of its six ethical principles, defining it as "fostering the practitioner's self-knowledge and care for self." One activity mentioned for fostering self-care is "seeking counselling or therapy and other opportunities for personal development as required." This activity is common among American psychologists, 90% of whom in one study reported participating in personal therapy at least once (Norcross & Rogan, 2013). It is incumbent on mental health care providers to proactively and routinely engage in self-care practices so as to be at their best and to provide quality care to their clients.

Preparing for the Future of Mental Health Counseling

Preparing new and future professionals for practice in mental health counseling (MHC) is a daunting task. So is preparing the field of mental health care for its future, a field that includes a variety of professions and providers, not just professional counselors. The challenges of developing and retaining a skillful mental health care workforce are much greater than ever before, and the stakes for not adapting to and participating in the transformation of a national mental health care delivery system are higher than even a few years ago. Recent federal legislation (namely, the PPACA) is, in essence, demanding major shifts in how mental health care is provided. Practitioners, educators, and supervisors from all disciplines must "limber up" so as to help fashion and guide such a systemic and professional transformation.

Given the forecasts of a transformed mental health care system, the formal preparation of future mental health care providers will necessarily undergo significant change. First and foremost, such training will become much more *integrative*. This means in part that professional or disciplinary divides will likely blur to a certain extent and a shared behavioral health care curriculum will be developed. This curriculum will feature extensive training in evidence-based practices (EBPs), will target methods for professional collaboration (e.g., how to work as a member of a treatment team), and will include content in business economics. Cummings and O'Donohue (2008) have emphasized the importance of mental health care providers being business- and economics-savvy in light of the "economic illiteracy" (p. 143) of current psychotherapists. They argue that because most health care dollars are *not* spent on mental health care, providers of MHC need to pursue more of the financial resources available so as to make mental health care more accessible and effective.

Second, the focus on *specialized training* (e.g., in EBPs) will be essential, moving beyond the same recycled approaches that have plagued the mental health field (Cummings & O'Donohue, 2008). EBPs (described earlier in this chapter) are essentially products of theoretical and therapeutic integrations: they are innovations that combine interventions from existing approaches, adapting them to target specific diagnostic and population groups. In an integrated and transformed mental health care system, EBP training will occur on-site and in the company of a range of professionals (e.g., nurses, psychiatrists, psychologists, professional counselors). Many of these sites will be hospital and primary care settings, sites that resemble the model of a "teaching hospital." To accommodate or be relevant for these settings and a professional collaborative structure, therapeutic approaches offered will undergo modification. These include the three that Alexander et al. (2013) describe: problem-solving therapy, CBT, and interpersonal therapy. These and other approaches will then be delivered in abbreviated sessions (e.g., 30 minutes) and over a short duration (4-6 sessions) so as to increase client engagement. Further expansion of delivery formats (e.g., individual, group) and methods (e.g., computer- or technology-based) will take place and will emphasize psychoeducation and self-management skills (e.g., coping).

Students in MHC preparation programs will likely be exposed much earlier to EBPs and practice settings (e.g., clinical shadowing or observation in the first semester), and clinicians already trained in an EBP will participate in ongoing supervision to monitor their adherence to the EBP, promote and maintain their skillfulness, and adapt the EBP to specific cultural groups. This type of training method will exemplify a learning-to-learn model, meaning that the pursuit of skillfulness is a perpetual task that requires adaptations in learning (e.g., willingness to be audio recorded and to receive feedback). The projected increase in clinician oversight or *ongoing supervision* reflects a third change forecasted in a transformed mental health care system.

A fourth and final anticipated change, related to the previous two, is that all mental health care practitioners will be expected to demonstrate their craft and to clearly define their product, something that has been a difficult task for far too long (Cummings & O'Donohue, 2008). This means in part supplying funding sources and other stakeholders (e.g., community leaders, citizens who vote and pay taxes) with credible and convincing data about the benefits of MHC, outcomes such as improved physical health, employment accessibility and stability, economic savings, and community safety and prosperity. In a nutshell, this fourth change constitutes *accountability*.

The future of MHC is one that is integrative, collaborative, evidence-based, accountable, and explicit. These are the characteristics of a transformed mental health care system. A daunting task, yes, and yet one that is necessary and also promising. Alexander et al. (2013, p. 209) warn that mental health professionals and primary care providers—and those who train them—who do not prepare for this type of a system will do so "at their peril." It is for those who struggle with a wide range of mental health concerns and conditions—and their families and communities—that preparation efforts are worth it.

Chapter Summary

It is important to reiterate at the close of this chapter that mental health counseling (MHC) has been defined here as an inclusive, interdisciplinary practice, one that is not restricted to professional counselors or to any other group of practitioners. This broad application includes the methods of psychotherapy (sometimes referred to as "talk therapy") *and* psychopharmacology. The combination of these two methods will soon be referred to consistently as *behavioral health care*, and as distinctions among mental health care professionals fade, those who provide these services will be known collectively as *behavioral health care providers*. Collaboration among providers will become increasingly routine for the purpose of delivering comprehensive, coordinated, and seamless care.

These projections "paint the face" of MHC in the 21st century in the United States. After more than a century of professional division and splintering within the mental health care field (i.e., the creation of specialty professions, e.g., psychology, counseling), it seems appropriate that movement in the next century is toward unification, or at least heightened collaboration. Clients and persons with unmet needs deserve cohesive care, care that prevents them from "falling through the cracks." In the transformed and integrated mental health care system, there are no "cracks." This is the ideal, yes, and one worth the dedication and perseverance of professionals who choose to enter at this exciting and promising time, and those who remain champions of relevant and effective care.

Resources

Various websites are provided throughout this chapter for information related to national survey research data on mental health, evidence-based practices, ethical guidelines, and current federal legislation on health care. Three additional websites are presented here, and are resources providing information on specialized services.

- Defense Centers of Excellence for Psychological Health and Traumatic Brain Injury, funded/sponsored in part by the U.S. Department of Defense: www.dcoe.mil
- Crisis Intervention Team (CIT) International, organization designed to promote CIT programs (collaborations among law enforcement, mental health care providers, persons with mental illness and their families and communities) and reduce the stigma of mental illness in the United States and in other countries: http://citinternational.org
- Suicide Prevention Resource Center: www.sprc.org

Practice Activities

1. Describe the two-pronged purpose of mental health counseling (MHC). How has this purpose changed over the years? How have political, societal, and national and world events (e.g., war, natural disasters) changed the delivery of MHC over the past 100 to 150 years?
2. Select one trend or priority of MHC from the seven presented and discussed in one section of this chapter and pair it with one of the six target populations or concerns in MHC discussed in another section. How would the one trend or priority you have selected be addressed with the one target population or concern you have selected? For example, how might co-occurring disorders be addressed in young adults and/or racial/ethnic minorities? Or, what services settings need to be considered in providing care to older adults and their families?
3. Identify two key practices of MHC presented in this chapter that remain relatively new and unexplored for you. With a peer or supervisor, discuss specific action steps that can be taken to implement aspects of these key practices in your current practice setting and community. For example, what specific marketing tasks can be employed realistically to correct misperceptions of mental illness and MHC among "untapped" populations in your community, that is, those with unmet needs? How would these tasks exemplify the five ethical principles mentioned in this chapter?

References

Ægisdóttir, S., O'Heron, M. P., Hartong, J. M., Haynes, S. A., & Linville, M. K. (2011). Enhancing attitudes and reducing fears about mental health counseling: An analogue study. *Journal of Mental Health Counseling, 33*, 327-346.

Alexander, C. L., Arnkoff, D. B., & Glass, C. R. (2010). Bringing psychotherapy to primary care: Innovations and challenges. *Clinical Psychology: Science and Practice, 17*, 191-214.

American Counseling Association. (2014). *ACA Code of Ethics*. Alexandria, VA: Author.

American Psychiatric Association. (1980). *Diagnostic and statistical manual of mental disorders* (3rd ed.). Washington, DC: Author.

American Psychiatric Association. (2000). *Diagnostic and statistical manual of mental disorders* (4th ed., text revision). Washington, DC: Author.

American Psychological Association. (2010). *Mental health insurance under the federal parity law*. Retrieved from http://www.apa.org/helpcenter/federal-parity-law.aspx

Anker, M. G., Duncan, B. L., & Sparks, J. A. (2009). Using client feedback to improve couple therapy outcomes: A randomized clinical trial in a naturalistic setting. *Journal of Consulting and Clinical Psychology, 77*, 693-704.

APA Presidential Task Force on Evidence-based Practice. (2006). Evidence-based practice in psychology. *American Psychologist, 61*, 271-285.

Blount, A. (Ed.). (1998). *Integrated primary care: The future of medical and mental health collaboration*. New York: W. W. Norton.

Boyer, S. L., & Bond, G. R. (1999). Does assertive community treatment reduce burnout? A comparison with traditional case management. *Mental Health Services Research, 1*, 31-45.

Brems, C., & Johnson, M. E. (1997). Clinical implications of the occurrence of substance use and other psychiatric disorders. *Professional Psychology: Research and Practice, 28*, 437-447.

Burns, B. J., Costello, E. J., Angold, A., Tweed, D., Stangl, D., Farmer, E. M., & Erkanli, A. (1995). Children's mental health service use across service sectors. *Health Affairs, 14*, 147-159.

Butler, J. R., & Hyler, S. E. (2005). Hollywood portrayals of child and adolescent mental health treatment: Implications for clinical practice. *Child and Adolescent Psychiatric Clinics of North America, 14*, 509-522.

Carlat, D. (2010). *Unhinged: The trouble with psychiatry—A doctor's revelations about a profession in crisis*. New York: Free Press.

Cautin, R. L. (2011). A century of psychotherapy, 1860-1960. In J. C. Norcross, G. R. VandenBos, & D. K. Freedheim (Eds.), *History of psychotherapy: Continuity and change* (2nd ed.; pp. 3-38). Washington, DC: American Psychological Association.

Chae, D. H., & Ayala, G. (2010). Sexual orientation and sexual behavior among Latino and Asian Americans: Implications for unfair treatment and psychological distress. *Journal of Sex Research, 47*, 451-459.

Chen, J., & Rizzo, J. (2010). Racial and ethnic disparities in use of psychotherapy: Evidence from U.S. national survey data. *Psychiatric Services, 61*, 364-372.

Compton, M. T., Neubert, B. N. D., Broussard, B., McGriff, J. A., Morgan, R., & Oliva, J. R. (2011). Use of force preferences and perceived effectiveness of actions among Crisis

Intervention Team (CIT) police officers and non-CIT officers in an escalating psychiatric crisis involving a subject with schizophrenia. *Schizophrenia Bulletin, 37,* 737-745.

Corey, G., Corey, M. S., Corey, C., & Callanan, P. (2015). *Issues and ethics in the helping professions* (9th ed.). Stamford, CT: Cengage Learning.

Corrigan, P. (2004). How stigma interferes with mental health care. *American Psychologist, 59,* 614-625.

Corrigan, P., Markowitz, F. E., & Watson, A. C. (2004). Structural levels of mental illness stigma and discrimination. *Schizophrenia Bulletin, 30,* 481-491.

Corrigan, P. W. (2011). Strategic stigma change (SSC): Five principles for social marketing campaigns to reduce stigma. *Psychiatric Services, 62,* 824-826.

Corrigan, P. W., Morris, S. B., Michaels, P. J., Rafacz, J. D., & Rüsch, N. (2012). Challenging the public stigma of mental illness: A meta-analysis of outcome studies. *Psychiatric Services, 63,* 963-973.

Cummings, J. R., Lucas, S. M., & Druss, B. G. (2013). Addressing public stigma and disparities among persons with mental illness: The role of federal policy. *American Journal of Public Health, 103,* 781-785.

Cummings, N. A., & Cummings, J. L. (2013). *Refocused psychotherapy as the first line intervention in behavioral health.* New York: Routledge.

Cummings, N. A., Cummings, J. L., & Johnson, J. N. (Eds.). (1997). *Behavioral health in primary care: A guide for clinical integration.* Madison, CT: Psychosocial Press.

Cummings, N. A., & O'Donohue, W. T. (2008). *Eleven blunders that cripple psychotherapy in America: A remedial unblundering.* New York: Routledge.

Cummings, N., O'Donohue, W., Hayes, S. C., & Follette, V. (2001). *Integrated behavioral healthcare: Positioning mental health practice with medical/surgical practice.* San Diego, CA: Academic Press.

Cutler, D. L., Sills, G. M., Svendsen, D., & Yeager, K. R. (2013). Public mental health in America: "Enlightenment" to accountable care. In K. R. Yeager, D. L. Cutler, D. Svendsen, & G. M. Sills (Eds.), *Modern community mental health: An interdisciplinary approach* (pp. 8-27). New York: Oxford University Press.

Davis, T. F., & Biltz, G. R. (1998). Forming a multidisciplinary team. In A. Blount (Ed.), *Integrated primary care: The future of medical and mental health collaboration* (pp. 228-246). New York: W. W. Norton.

DeLeon, P. H., Kenkel, M. B., Garcia-Shelton, L., & VandenBos, G. R. (2011). Psychotherapy, 1960 to the present. In J. C. Norcross, G. R. VandenBos, & D. K. Freedheim (Eds.), *History of psychotherapy: Continuity and change* (2nd ed.; pp. 39-62). Washington, DC: American Psychological Association.

DeLuca, N. L., Moser, L. L., & Bond, G. R. (2008). Assertive community treatment. In K. T. Mueser & D. V. Jeste (Eds.), *Clinical handbook of schizophrenia* (pp. 329-338). New York: Guilford Press.

DeViva, J. (in press). Treatment utilization among OEF/OIF veterans referred for psychotherapy for PTSD. *Psychological Services.* DOI: 10.1037/a0035077

Duckworth, K. (2013). *Mental health professionals: Who they are and how to find one.* Retrieved from http://www.nami.org/Content/ContentGroups/Helpline1/Mental_Health_ Professionals_Who_They_Are_and_How_to_Find_One.htm

Dyches, H., Biegel, D. E., Johnsen, J. A., Guo, S., & Min, M. O. (2002). The impact of mobile crisis services on the use of community-based mental health services. *Research on Social Work Practice, 12*, 731-751.

Eisenberg, D., Hunt, J., & Speer, N. (2013). Mental health in American colleges and universities: Variation across student subgroups and across campuses. *Journal of Nervous and Mental Disease, 201*, 60-67.

Everett, A., & Lee, S. Y. (2012). Community and public mental health services in the United States: History and programs. In W. W. Eaton (Ed.), *Public mental health* (pp. 396-414). New York: Oxford University Press.

Fong, M. L. (1990). Mental health counseling: The essence of professional counseling. *Counselor Education & Supervision, 30*, 106-113.

Frueh, B. C., Ford, J. D., Elhai, J. D., & Grubaugh, A. L. (2012). Evidence-based practice in adult mental health. In P. Sturmey & M. Hersen (Eds.), *Handbook of evidence-based practice in clinical psychology, Volume 2: Adult disorders* (pp. 3-14). Hoboken, NJ: Wiley.

Fullerton, C. A., Busch, A. B., Normand, S. L., McGuire, T. G., & Epstein, A. M. (2011). Ten-year trends in quality of care and spending for depression: 1996 through 2005. *Archives of General Psychiatry, 68*, 1218-1226.

Glosoff, H. L., & Schwarz-Whittaker, J. E. (2013). The counseling profession: Historical perspectives and current issues and trends. In D. Capuzzi & D. R. Gross (Eds.), *Introduction to the counseling profession* (6th ed.; pp. 30-76). New York: Routledge.

Golberstein, E., Eisenberg, D., & Gollust, S. E. (2008). Perceived stigma and mental health care seeking. *Psychiatric Services, 59*, 392-399.

Granello, D. H. (2013). Addressing suicide risk in community mental health. In K. R. Yeager, D. L. Cutler, D. Svendsen, & G. M. Sills (Eds.), *Modern community mental health: An interdisciplinary approach* (pp. 433-452). New York, NY: Oxford University Press.

Guo, S., Biegel, D. E., Johnsen, J. A., & Dyches, H. (2001). Assessing the impact of community-based mobile crisis services on preventing hospitalization. *Psychiatric Services, 52*, 223-228.

Henggeler, S. W. (2001). Multisystemic therapy. *Residential Treatment for Children and Youth, 18*, 75-85.

Hu, G., Wilcox, H. C., Wissow, L., & Baker, S. P. (2008). Mid-life suicide: An increasing problem in U.S. Whites, 1999-2005. *American Journal of Preventive Medicine, 35*, 589-593.

Humes, K. R., Jones, N. A., & Ramirez, R. R. (2011, March). Overview of race and Hispanic origin: 2010 [2010 Census Briefs]. U.S. Census Bureau. Accessible at http://www.census.gov/2010census/

Hunter, C. L., Goodie, J. L., Oordt, M. S., & Dobmeyer, A. C. (2009). *Integrated behavioral health in primary care: Step-by-step guidance for assessment and intervention.* Washington, DC: American Psychological Association.

Kaltman, S., de Mendoza, A. H., Gonzales, F. A., & Serrano, A. (in press). Preferences for trauma-related mental health services among Latina immigrants from Central America, South America, and Mexico. *Psychological Trauma: Theory, Research, Practice, and Policy.* DOI: 10.1037/a0031539

Kasick, D. P., & Bowling, C. D. (2013). Crisis intervention teams: A boundary-spanning collaboration between the law enforcement and mental health communities.

In K. R. Yeager, D. L. Cutler, D. Svendsen, & G. M. Sills (Eds.). (2013). *Modern community mental health: An interdisciplinary approach* (pp. 304-315). New York: Oxford University Press.

Kessler, R. C., Demler, O., Frank, R. G., Olfson, M., Pincus, H. A., Walters, E. E., Wang, P., Wells, K. B., & Zaslavsky, A. M. (2005a). Prevalence and treatment of mental disorders, 1990 to 2003. *New England Journal of Medicine, 352*, 2525-2523.

Kessler, R. C., Berglund, P., Demler, O., Jin, R., Merikangas, K. R., & Walters, E. E. (2005b). Lifetime prevalence and age-of-onset distributions of DSM-IV disorders in the National Comorbidity Survey Replication. *Archives of General Psychiatry, 62*, 593-603.

Kessler, R. C., Heeringa, S., Lakoma, N. D., Petukhova, M., Rupp, A. E., Schoenbaum, M., Wang, P. S., & Zaslavsky, A. M. (2008). Individual and societal effects of mental disorders on earnings in the United States: Results from the National Comorbidity Survey Replication. *American Journal of Psychiatry, 165*, 703-711.

Kiluk, B. D., Sugarman, D. E., Nich, C., Gibbons, C. J., Martino, S., Rounsaville, B. J., & Carroll, K. M. (2011). A methodological analysis of randomized clinical trials of computer-assisted therapies for psychiatric disorders: Toward improved standards for an emerging field. *American Journal of Psychiatry, 168*, 790-799.

Knudsen, H. K., Ducharme, L. J., & Roman, P. M. (2008). Clinical supervision, emotional exhaustion, and turnover intention: A study of substance abuse treatment counselors in the Clinical Trials Network on the National Institute on Drug Abuse. *Journal of Substance Abuse Treatment, 35*, 387-395.

Kosovski, J. R., & Smith, D. C. (2011). Everybody hurts: Addiction, drama, and the family in the reality television show Intervention. *Substance Use & Misuse, 46*, 852-858.

Kraft, D. P. (2009). *Mens sana*: The growth of mental health in the American College Health Association. *Journal of American College Health, 58*, 267-275.

Kuehn, B. M. (2010). Military probes epidemic of suicide: Mental health issues remain prevalent. *JAMA, 304*(13), 1427-1430.

Lambert, M. J. (1992). Psychotherapy outcome research: Implications for integrative and eclectic psychotherapists. In J. C. Norcross & M. R. Goldfried (Eds.), *Handbook of psychotherapy integration* (pp. 94-129). New York: Basic Book.

Lambert, M. J. (2010). *Prevention of treatment failure: The use of measuring, monitoring, and feedback in clinical practice*. Washington, DC: American Psychological Association.

Larkin, G. L., Smith, R. P., & Beautrais, A. L. (2008). Trends in US emergency department visits for suicide attempts, 1992-2001. *Crisis, 29*, 73-80.

Ledoux, T., Barnett, M. D., Garcini, L. M., & Baker, J. (2009). Predictors of recent mental health service use in a medical population: Implications for integrated care. *Journal of Clinical Psychology in Medical Settings, 16*, 304-310.

Leis, J. A., Mendelson, T., Perry, D. F., & Tandon, D. (2011). Perceptions of mental health services among low-income, perinatal African-American women. *Women's Health Issues, 21*, 314-319.

Li, Y. (2010). Provision of mental health services in U.S. nursing homes, 1995-2004. *Psychiatric Services, 61*, 349-355.

Lindsey, M. A., Brandt, N. E., Becker, K. D., Lee, B. R., Barth, R. P., Daleiden, E. L., & Chorpita, B. F. (in press). Identifying the common elements of treatment engagement interventions in children's mental health services. *Clinical Child and Family Psychology Review*. DOI 10.1007/s10567-013-0163-x

López-Muñoz, F., Alamo, C., Cuenca, E., Shen, W. W., Clervoy, P., & Rubio, G. (2005). History of the discovery and clinical introduction of chlorpromazine. *Annals of Clinical Psychiatry, 17*, 113-135.

Lowry, R., Crosby, A. E., Brener, N. D., & Kann, L. (2014). Suicidal thoughts and attempts among U.S. high school students: Trends and associated health-risk behaviors, 1991-2011. *Journal of Adolescent Health, 54*, 100-108.

Lucock, M. P., Hall, P., & Noble, R. (2006). A survey of influences on the practice of psychotherapists and clinical psychologists in training in the UK. *Clinical Psychology and Psychotherapy, 13*, 123-130.

Manderscheid, R. (in press). The Affordable Care Act: Overview and implications for county and city behavioral health and intellectual/developmental disability programs. *Journal of Social Work in Disability & Rehabilitation*. DOI 10.1080/1536710X.2013.870510

Manuel, J. I., Appelbaum, P. S., Le Melle, S. M., Mancini, A. D., Huz, S., Stellato, C. B., & Finnerty, M. T. (2013). Use of intervention strategies by assertive community treatment teams to promote patients' engagement. *Psychiatric Services, 64*, 579-585.

Martins, S. S., Ko, J., Kuwabara, S., Clarke, D., Alexandre, P., Zandi, P., Mendelson, T., Mortensen, P. B., & Eaton, W. W. (2012). The relationship of adult mental disorders to socioeconomic status, race/ethnicity, marital status, and urbanicity of residence. In In W. Eaton & the Faculty, Students, and Fellows of the Department of Mental Health, Bloomberg School of Public Health (Eds.), *Public mental health* (pp. 151-197). New York, NY: Oxford University Press.

McCarthy, J. F., Valenstein, M., Kim, H. M., Ilgen, M., Zivin, K., & Blow, F. C. (2009). Suicide mortality among patients receiving care in the Veterans health administration health system. *American Journal of Epidemiology, 169*, 1033-1038.

McCrady, B. S., Epstein, E. E., Cook, S., Jensen, N. K., & Ladd, B. O. (2011). What do women want? Alcohol treatment choices, treatment entry and retention. *Psychology of Addictive Behaviors, 25*, 521-529.

McLaughlin, K. A., Koenen, K. C., Hill, E. D., Petukhova, M., Sampson, N. A., Zaslavsky, A. M., & Kessler, R. C. (2013). Trauma exposure and posttraumatic stress disorder in a national sample of adolescents. *Journal of the American Academy of Child & Adolescent Psychiatry, 52*, 815-830.

Miller, W. R., & Carroll, K. M. (2006). Drawing science together: Ten principles, ten recommendations. In W. R. Miller & K. M. Carroll (Eds.), *Rethinking substance abuse: What the science shows, and what we should do about it* (pp. 293-311). New York: Guilford Press.

Miller, W. R., & Rollnick, S. (2013). *Motivational interviewing: Helping people change*. New York: Guilford Press.

Milne, D. (2009). *Evidence-based clinical supervision: Principles and practice*. Chichester, West Sussex, UK: Wiley-Blackwell.

Mott, J. M., Barrera, T. L., Hernandez, C., Graham, D. P., & Teng, E. J. (2014). Rates and predictors of referral for individual psychotherapy, group psychotherapy, and medications among Iraq and Afghanistan veterans with PTSD. *Journal of Behavioral Health Services & Research, 41*, 99-109.

Mudford, O. C., McNeill, R., Walton, L., & Phillips, K. J. (2012). Rationale and standards of evidence-based practice. In P. Sturmey & M. Hersen (Eds.), *Handbook of evidence-based practice in clinical psychology, Volume 1: Child and adolescent disorders* (pp. 3-26). Hoboken, NJ: Wiley.

Mueser, K. T., & Drake, R. E. (2007). Comorbidity: What have we learned and where are we going? *Clinical Psychology: Science and Practice, 14*, 64-69.

Nadeem, E., Lange, J. M., & Miranda, J. (2008). Mental health care preferences among low-income and minority women. *Archives of Women's Mental Health, 11*, 93-102.

National Center for Veterans Analysis and Statistics. (2013). Profile of Veterans: 2011: Data from the American Community Survey. Accessible at http://www1.va.gov/vetdata/docs/SpecialReports/Profile_of_Veterans_2011.pdf

New Freedom Commission on Mental Health. (2003). *Achieving the Promise: Transforming Mental Health Care in America, Final Report*. DHHS Pub. No. SMA-03-3832. Rockville, MD: U.S. Department of Health and Human Services.

Norcross, J. C., & Rogan, J. D. (2013). Psychologists conducting psychotherapy in 2012: Current practices and historical trends among Division 29 members. *Psychotherapy, 50*, 490-495.

Nunes, D., Daly, B., Rao, K., Borntrager, C., Chambers, K. L., Rohner, K., & Shrestha, S. (2010). Technology in child and adolescent and school mental health: A look at today and tomorrow. *Advances in School Mental Health Promotion, 3*(3), 26-35.

Nystul, M. S. (2011). *Introduction to counseling: An art and science perspective*. Upper Saddle River, NJ: Pearson Education.

Olfson, M., & Marcus, S. C. (2010). National trends in outpatient psychotherapy. *American Journal of Psychiatry, 167*, 1456-1463.

Orlinksy, D. E., Botermans, J., Rønnestad, M. H., & the SPR Collaborative Research Network. (2001). Towards an empirically grounded model of psychotherapy training: Four thousand therapists rate influences on their development. *Australian Psychologist, 36*, 139-148.

Owen, J., Devdas, L., & Rodolfa, E. (2007). University counseling center off-campus referrals: An exploratory investigation. *Journal of College Student Psychotherapy, 22*, 13-29.

Pearlman, S. A. (2013). The Patient Protection and Affordable Care Act: Impact on mental health services and demand and provider availability. *Journal of the American Psychiatric Nurses Association, 19*, 327-334.

Phelan, J. C., Bromet, E. J., & Link, B. G. (1998). Psychiatric illness and family stigma. *Schizophrenia Bulletin, 24*, 115-126.

Pope, K. S., & Vasquez, M. J. T. (2011). *Ethics in psychotherapy and counseling: A practical guide* (4th ed.). Hoboken, NJ: John Wiley & Sons.

Reeves, A., Stuckler, D., McKee, M., Gunnell, D., Chang, S., & Basu, S. (2012). Increase in state suicide rates in the USA during economic recession. *The Lancet, 380*, 1813-1814.

Remley, T. P., Jr., & Herlihy, B. (2014). *Ethical, legal, and professional issues in counseling* (4th ed.). Boston, MA: Pearson Education.

Roll, J. M., Kennedy, J., Tran, M., & Howell, D. (2013). Disparities in unmet need for mental health services in the United States: 1997-2010. *Psychiatric Services, 64*, 80-82.

Rosen, A., Mueser, K. T., & Teesson, M. (2007). Assertive community treatment – Issues from scientific and clinical literature with implications for practice. *Journal of Rehabilitation Research & Development, 44*, 813-826.

Rosen, C. S., Greenbaum, M. A., Fitt, J. E., Laffaye, C., Norris, V. A., & Kimerling, R. (2011). Stigma, help-seeking attitudes, and use of psychotherapy in veterans with diagnoses of posttraumatic stress disorder. *Journal of Nervous and Mental Disease, 199*, 879-885.

Rosenthal, R. N. (2013). Treatment of persons with substance use disorder and co-occurring other mental disorders. In B. S. McCrady & E. E. Epstein (Eds.), *Addictions: A comprehensive guidebook* (pp. 559-707). New York: Oxford University Press.

Ryan, M., Nitsun, M., Gilbert, L., & Mason, H. (2005). A prospective study of the effectiveness of group and individual psychotherapy for women CSA survivors. *Psychology and Psychotherapy: Theory, Research and Practice, 78*, 465-479.

Salzer, M. S., Schwenk, E., & Brusilovskiy, E. (2010). Certified peer specialist roles and activities: Results from a national survey. *Psychiatric Services, 61*, 520-523.

Schauman, O. Aschan, L. E., Arias, N., Beards, S. & Clement, S. (2013). Interventions to increase initial appointment attendance in mental health services: A systematic review. *Psychiatric Services, 64*, 1249-1258.

Schmidt, L. T., Pinninti, N. R., Garfinkle, B., & Solomon, P. (2013). Assertive community treatment teams. In K. R. Yeager, D. L. Cutler, D. Svendsen, & G. M. Sills (Eds.), *Modern community mental health: An interdisciplinary approach* (pp. 293-303). New York: Oxford University Press.

Scott, R. L. (2000). Evaluation of a mobile crisis program: Effectiveness, efficiency, and consumer satisfaction. *Psychiatric Services, 51*, 1153-1156.

Simon, G. E., Imel, Z. E., Ludman, E. J., & Steinfeld, B. J. (2012). Is dropout after a first psychotherapy visit always a bad outcome? *Psychiatric Services, 63*, 705-707.

Smith, T. E., Burgos, J., Dexter, V., Norcott, J., Pappas, S. V., Shuman, E., Appel, A., Harrison, M. E., Nossel, I. R., & Essock, S. M. (2010). Best practices for improving engagement of clients in clinic care. *Psychiatric Services, 61*, 343-345.

Sperry, L. (2013). Integrated behavioral health: Implications for individual and family counseling practice. *The Family Journal, 21*, 347-350.

Spruill, D. A., & Fong, M. L. (1990). Defining the domain of mental health counseling: From identity confusion to consensus. *Journal of Mental Health Counseling, 12*, 12-23.

State Medicaid Director Letter on Peer Support Services. (2007, August). SMDL 07-011. Baltimore, Centers for Medicare and Medicaid Services. Available at www.cms.hhs.gov/SMDL/downloads/SMD081507A.pdf

Stevens, L. F., & Henrie, D. D. (1966). A history of psychiatric nursing. *Bulletin of the Menninger Clinic, 30*, 32-38.

Storr, C. L., Azur, M., Bass, J. K., & Wilcox, H. C. (2012). Adapting to acute crisis. In W. Eaton & The Faculty, Students, and Fellows of the Department of Mental Health, Bloomberg School of Public Health (Eds.), *Public mental health* (pp. 303-347). New York, NY: Oxford University Press.

Strassle, C. G., Borckardt, J. J., Handler, L., & Nash, M. (2011). Video-tape role induction for psychotherapy: Moving forward. *Psychotherapy, 48*, 170-178.

Strosahl, K. (2001). The integration of primary care and behavioral health: Type II change in the era of managed care. In N. Cummings, W. O'Donohue, S. Hayes, & V. Follette (Eds.), *Integrated behavioral healthcare: Positioning mental health practice with medical/surgical practice* (pp. 45-69). London, UK: Academic Press.

Substance Abuse and Mental Health Services Administration (SAMHSA). (2005). *Substance Abuse Treatment for Persons with Co-Occurring Disorders.* Treatment Improvement Protocol (TIP) Series, No. 42. HHS Publication No. (SMA) 133992. Rockville, MD: SAMHSA.

Substance Abuse and Mental Health Services Administration (SAMHSA). (2012). *Mental Health, United States, 2010.* HHS Publication No. (SMA) 12-4681. Rockville, MD: SAMHSA.

Substance Abuse and Mental Health Services Administration (SAMHSA). (2013). *Results from the 2012 National Survey on Drug Use and Health: Mental Health Findings.* (NSDUH Series H-47). HHS Publication No. (SMA) 13-4805. Rockville, MD: SAMHSA.

Sue, D. W., & Sue, D. (2008). *Counseling the culturally diverse: Theory and practice* (5th ed.). Hoboken, NJ: Wiley.

Swift, J. K., Greenberg, R. P., Whipple, J. L., & Kominiak, N. (2012). Practice recommendations for reducing premature termination in therapy. *Professional Psychology: Research and Practice, 43*, 379-387.

Torrey, E. F. (1997). *Out of the shadows: Confronting America's mental illness crisis.* New York: John Wiley.

U.S. Department of Health and Human Services. (1999). *Mental health: A report of the Surgeon General.* Rockville, MD: Author.

U.S. Department of Health and Human Services. (2001). *Mental health: Culture, race, and ethnicity – A supplement to Mental health: A report of the Surgeon General.* Rockville, MD: Author.

U.S. Department of Health and Human Services. (2012). *2012 National Strategy for Suicide Prevention: Goals and Objectives for Action.* Washington, DC: Author.

Vessey, J. T., & Howard, K. I. (1990). Who seeks psychotherapy? *Psychotherapy, 30*, 546-553.

Vick, B., Jones, K., & Mitra, S. (2012). Poverty and severe psychiatric disorder in the U.S.: Evidence from the Medical Expenditure Panel Survey. *Journal of Mental Health Policy and Economics, 15*, 83-96.

Watkins, D. C., Hunt, J. B., & Eisenberg, D. (2011). Increased demand for mental health services on college campuses: Perspectives from administrators. *Qualitative Social Work, 11*, 319-337.

Watson, A. C., & Fulambarker, A. J. (2012). The crisis intervention team model of police response to mental health crises: A primer for mental health practitioners. *Best Practices in Mental Health, 8*, 71-81.

Watson, A. C., Ottati, V. C., Morabito, M. J., Draine, J., Kerr, A. N., & Angell, B. (2010). Outcomes of police contacts with persons with mental illness: The impact of CIT. *Administration & Policy in Mental Health, 37*, 302-317.

Weikel, W. J., & Palmo, A. J. (1989). The evolution and practice of mental health counseling. *Journal of Mental Health Counseling, 11*, 7-25.

Welfel, E. R. (2013). *Ethics in counseling and psychotherapy: Standards, research, and emerging issues* (5th ed.). Belmont, CA: Brooks/Cole—Cengage Learning.

Whitaker, R. (2010). *Anatomy of an epidemic: Magic bullets, psychiatric drugs, and the astonishing rise of mental illness in America.* New York: Crown Publishers.

Yeager, K. R., Cutler, D. L., Svendsen, D., & Sills, G. M. (Eds.). (2013). *Modern community mental health: An interdisciplinary approach.* New York: Oxford University Press.

Yu, J. W., Adams, S. H., Burns, J., Brindis, C. D., & Irwin, C. E. (2008). Use of mental health counseling as adolescents become young adults. *Journal of Adolescent Health, 43*, 268-276.